ACKNOWLEDGMENTS

My husband BILL - Thank you for always being there for me and loving me the way you do. You are my hero.

My daughters KELLIE, RACHEL and JENNA - Thanks my angels for being so supportive and letting your Mum create her second dream. I know it has been hard for you sometimes when I am away from home but always know that you three beautiful girls are my everything.

My sister LINDA - Thank you for thinking of the title SYMPLY TOO GOOD TO BE TRUE, you are such a sweetie and I love you lots.

My mum FAY and sister LEONIE - My No.1 fans. I can't thank you both enough for your support and encouragement. You are so special and I love you lots.

Photographer SALLY HAXTON - Thank you once again for doing the photos in my new cookbook. I love working with you and am in awe at your ability to know what I want and how to make it come to life on film. You are just the best. Ph: (07) 5474 9129.

Food stylist BILL SYM - Not only are you the best husband in the world but a truly gifted chef. You did a terrific job making my recipes look so wonderful for the photo shoot.

Dietitian LISA COCHRANE - from Diabetes Australia Victoria. I am indebted to you for your outstanding contribution to this cookbook.

My printer THE INK SPOT, Maroochydore - To John and his wonderful team. Thank you once again for doing such an outstanding job. I didn't want anyone else but you to print my cookbooks. Why settle for anything less than the best. Thank you. Ph: (07) 5443 5431.

Graphics CHILLI DESIGNS - To Darren and team. I really enjoy working with you. Your creative ideas are the best. Ph: (07) 5437 7788.

The kitchen store HOUSE - Thank you Leanne, Tina and staff at HOUSE in Kawana. For enquiries to HOUSE stores nationally Ph: (03) 9347 9244. Also thank you to Myer for supplying some of the crockery.

My distributors NETWORK SERVICES - Thank you to Mark, Cheryl and terrific staff. Because of your belief in my book I have achieved more than I could ever have hoped for. I am very grateful that I have you as my distributors - we have only begun!!

My promotional assistants TREVOR and JEANETTE - You are amazing friends, always there for me offering help and support whenever I need it. You both do a wonderful job with all the in-store promotions and make it so much fun. I can't thank you both enough.

My seminar assistant ANGI - Thank you honey for your friendship and enthusiasm. I enjoy having you with me on the seminar trail and really appreciate your help. I could not have done them without you and your caring ways.

My personal assistant JAN - I appreciate all the hard work that you did and for being there to offer your help wherever needed. Having you here has been wonderful. Thank you for your support and friendship.

My wonderful FAMILY and FRIENDS - You support me unconditionally. I am so blessed to have such loving and caring people in my life. I thank you for always being there for me. You know who you are; remember I value every one of you.

A big hug and a kiss to EVERYONE who has been involved in helping me make my second dream come true - SYMPLY TOO GOOD TO BE TRUE 2 .

Thank you everyone from the bottom of my healthy heart.

♡ Annette

CON~~TENTS~~

Welcome Back

Welcome back........to my world of tasty low-fat cooking! I am so excited to be sharing with you more of my favourite recipes and secrets to reducing the fats in cooking and showing you more ways to have tasty low-fat meals.

You now have my UPDATED VERSION published in 2005. The reason I have updated this cookbook was due to the many changes that have taken place with nutrition in the last few years. I felt it important to keep up with these changes, so you now have an all new and more informative version of SYMPLY TOO GOOD TO BE TRUE 2. With a new style and layout, plus some new photos this book now has a more modern look.

You will also find the nutritional panel at the bottom of each recipe now has SATURATED FATS, SUGAR, SODIUM and the GI RATING. Dietitian Lisa Cochrane from Diabetes Australia Victoria has written new and updated tips for each recipe and I have also checked every recipe and made some changes to those that needed to be healthier. Some recipes were too high in sodium (salt) and too high in carbohydrates so the changes I feel were important. Since I launched book 2 back in 1999 we have become more conscious of how much sodium we have in our diet and everyone is looking at lowering how many carbohydrates they have in their diet, which is why I felt it was important to make my recipes the best they can be - enjoy my new UPDATED VERSION.

So many diabetics have told me how much my first cookbook has helped them so I hope this information will be of value. You will notice the 'Dietitian's Tips" which were written by Lisa Cochrane specifically for people with diabetes. Because so many wonderful people have phoned, written or told me how much my book has helped them I have included a page of testimonials. - I keep every letter and treasure them.

Remember my story? I was a chubby child, cuddly teenager, buxom bride and an obese adult, at my heaviest weighing 100 kilos. I learnt how to finally have GUILT-FREE low-fat food and the rest is history. In my new cookbook you can now enjoy low-fat sausage rolls, macaroni cheese and apple pie to name but a few - bliss in every mouthful. All I have taken out of these traditional recipes is the fat, but kept in all the flavour. All the ingredients in the recipes can be purchased at your supermarket and once again they are so simple to make and taste good enough to delight all the family.

As you can see by my photo on the opposite page. There has been two Annette's. The old Annette at 100 kilos and the new me at 65 kilos. The old Annette's photo was taken in January, 1992. I remember how bad I felt about myself then - I felt really unwell, no energy, hated wearing fat clothes and worse still was gaining weight daily. The new me has been 65 kilos since 1993 and I have turned a totally negative aspect of my life and made it into the most positive experience. All because I was sick of being fat and decided to stop dieting....yes stop dieting.

Think about it, how many times have you lost weight only for it to find you again? I think in my lifetime I must have lost at least 500 kilos. Instead I decided to become a healthy person. What is a healthy person? To me it was someone who eats healthy, exercises, has energy, has vitality, is happy and bounces through the day, someone who has a lifestyle that they enjoy and that they can maintain their desired weight without too much difficulty, plus gets to wear nice clothes. That definitely was NOT me, that is until I made the decision to do whatever it would take to become healthy.

So that's what I did, I lost 35 kilos and have now kept that weight off ever since. We can all lose weight but what if you not only lost the weight but KEEP IT OFF FOR LIFE! Are you ready to get started? Here is what I did, firstly I decided that my eating habits had to change, I had to stop eating/bingeing on chocolates, chips and cakes late at night, secondly I got interested in low-fat cooking so that I could still have my cake but the healthy way. The best decision I made was to forget about all my past failures and begin again fresh and new, and with a confidence and belief in my ability to actually do this. I decided I was a healthy person and that was who I was going to be for the rest of my life. Here are 5 tips to help get you off the diet rollercoaster and become a healthy person:

1. Firstly BELIEVE IN YOURSELF, nothing will work if you don't have faith in yourself, or like yourself. Dieting does tend to destroy this, but have the faith. You can be the best you can be if you are willing to make some changes - changes to habits that have held you back in the past. These changes will benefit you for the rest of your life.

2. Once you stop depriving yourself of foods you like it is easier to make long term permanent changes that will make healthier lifestyle, using my cookbooks will help show you how to do this.

3. Look at how much fat you are eating in a day. Learn to choose the low-fat choices, cook low-fat, think low-fat and help avoid heart disease, high cholesterol, diabetes and even some cancers. You must learn how to not only lose weight but keep it off forever.

4. Set yourself small goals, achievable goals. Remember you didn't get this way overnight but if you stick with it and NEVER GIVE UP you will get where you want to be.

5. Be happy losing ½ to 1 kilo a week, losing weight too quickly you may find it will come back quickly. Take your time, teach yourself to make small changes, permanent changes. Believe me it will make a big difference long term.

The old Annette at 100 kilos and the healthy Annette at 65 kilos.

So spread the word - SYMPLY TOO GOOD TO BE TRUE 2   has arrived. Tell your family/friends, help them to become healthy too. I am sure you will enjoy cooking my way and see the fabulous results you can achieve and yet still enjoy your meals, no longer will you feel deprived and bored with what you eat. Come into my world and enjoy being the healthy person you deserve to be….I know you can do it!!

ENJOY EVERY MOUTHFUL!

Dietitian's Tips

Once more Annette has provided us with a selection of healthy and great tasting recipes that carry clear preparation instructions. Choosing to include these recipes in our everyday eating plan will make it easy to lose those extra kilograms or keep our weight where we want it - just right.

Latest figures tell us that around 60% of the adult population and 25% of children and adolescents are overweight or obese - and this figure is growing.

Why are we becoming the fat nation?

We simply have too much food that is kilojoule laden and high in fat and we don't move enough. All nations that have lots of food and plenty of money pile on the kilograms. History tells us that traditional societies did not have enough food or had to "feast and fast" to stay alive. Weight gain was not the issue; getting enough to eat was! How things have changed, and in many respects for the better. In Australia around a third of our money spent on food is on takeaways or in restaurants. Many of the serving sizes are enormous, and high in fat, sugar and kilojoules. Popular fast foods including hamburgers, fries and pizzas are high in fat, while soft drinks and many "fruit" drinks are high in sugar. Having these foods only occasionally or selecting the healthier alternatives from takeaways and restaurants are much healthier options. However the best option is to cook food yourself using fresh ingredients and following healthy recipes.

Eating to lose weight

Isn't it great that we now have two of Annette's cookbooks from which to select suitable recipes that allow us to eat healthily. These recipes can also be used for the whole family and will help us to lose weight. By selecting different recipes daily we will get a variety of food. This will help us feel fuller and more satisfied with what we eat, and generally stronger to continue with our goal of achieving a healthy weight.

Forget the high carbohydrate/low protein or high protein/low carbohydrate diet or the latest fad. The only way to lose weight and be healthy is to reduce the amount of total energy (kilojoules) in our eating plan and participate in regular physical activity. Fortunately Annette's recipes are lower in kilojoules than the traditional recipes.

Eating to live - healthier and longer

The latest research shows that many diseases we develop as we get older are due to our body weight and what we eat throughout our life. In the end we surely are what we eat. These chronic diseases include heart disease, diabetes and cancer. Fortunately we can reduce the risk of developing these conditions.

Preventing and managing heart disease

Heart disease is the leading cause of death in Australia. Food is directly involved in many of the risk factors for heart disease. Paying attention to what we eat is one of the most important preventative measures we can take. Coronary heart disease is caused by narrowing of the arteries in the walls of the heart. Fatty deposits cling to the artery walls and can clog the arteries, making it more likely that a blood clot will form. A heart attack occurs when a blood clot blocks one of the arteries of the heart. This prevents the flow of blood, cuts off the oxygen supply to the heart and damages or kills the heart cells.

Risk factors for heart disease include cigarette smoking, lack of physical activity and a family history of the disease. However the food-related risk factors include eating high saturated fat foods, being overweight or obese particularly if your weight is carried around your stomach rather than other areas of your body, and having high blood pressure.

Preventing and managing diabetes

Diabetes is a condition where the body's system for controlling blood glucose levels is not working properly. Either the body produces not enough insulin or the insulin it does produce isn't working properly. Without insulin, glucose cannot enter the cells. It builds up in the blood causing high blood glucose levels, starving the cells of energy. Uncontrolled diabetes and pre-diabetes can damage the artery walls and contribute to coronary heart disease, other blood vessel diseases, nerve damage, eye damage and kidney failure.

People who have Type 1 diabetes do not produce any insulin. This form of diabetes is not preventable and those who do have this must take insulin injections to live. A healthy eating plan along with insulin injections and physical activity will help these people to minimise the long-term effects of high blood glucose levels.

Some people initially have a condition called insulin resistance, where the insulin is produced in excess because the body is having difficulty using the normal amount required to take the glucose into the cells due to body fat affecting the cells. In insulin resistance the blood glucose level is OK, but eventually the pancreas gets tired of producing all the insulin and pre-diabetes can develop, where the blood glucose level is higher than in people without diabetes, but not as high as those with diabetes. If our body weight is not managed then we can develop Type 2 diabetes. Many people can prevent the development of Type 2 diabetes through healthy eating and physical activity. Research from Australia and around the world suggests that we can reduce the chance of developing Type 2 diabetes through eating healthy foods and being a healthy body weight.

Using the recipes in this book to achieve or maintain a healthy weight will decrease your chance of developing pre-diabetes and Type 2 diabetes. There is no special "diet" to prevent diabetes. Once more the advice from experts is to take a variety of foods, eat plenty of breads, cereals, fruits and vegetables, have some fat but with a low saturated fat intake, and maintain a healthy body weight by balancing physical activity and our food intake. We are fortunate that these are the principles that underlie the recipes in Annette's cookbooks.

Annette also includes the glycaemic index (GI) of her recipes. This may be of use to some people aiming to lose weight or to help control their diabetes. Low-GI foods that are high in fibre, including most fruits, vegetables and cereals, can be included in a healthy eating plan. These foods tend to cause a smaller and gradual rise in blood glucose than high-GI foods such as glucose lollies and white bread.

Preventing cancer

High-energy (kilojoules) and high-fat eating habits generally lead to becoming overweight or to obesity, and are thought to increase our risk of some cancers including breast cancer and prostate cancer. Plant-based eating plans high in fresh fruits, vegetables, legumes and whole grains may help to prevent these forms of cancer and bowel cancer.

To prevent cancers we need to take lots of protective anti-cancer vegetables, especially raw vegetables or salads, leafy green vegetables, carrots, tomatoes and citrus fruits. We also need to stop smoking, drink less alcohol and do some physical activity.

SYMPLY TOO GOOD TO BE TRUE 2
Fighting chronic disease

As a dietitian I am impressed that you have selected this cookbook to help manage your body weight. Your motivation may have been to present yourself better and look better. This is a great reason but your reward will be so much greater. This cookbook gives sound nutritional advice and practical ways to eat now and in the long term. These recipes contain abundant vegetables, are low in fat particularly saturated fat, add less sugar and minimise salt. These meals are symply too good to be true!

Lisa Cochrane
BSc. Grad Dip Diet.
MPH APD
Senior Dietitian
Diabetes Australia - Victoria

Dietitian's Tip
Look for these notes throughout the book for my tips & advice to assist people with diabetes.
Lisa Cochrane

THIS COOKBOOK HAS BEEN ENDORSED BY DIABETES AUSTRALIA

For any enquires phone Diabetes Australia on their toll free number

1300 136588

DIABETES AUSTRALIA

Annette's Tips

Breakfast

The MOST important meal of the day. If you find eating breakfast makes you feel sick, start with a glass of fresh juice or a piece of toast, then slowly add more. A cup of coffee (and a cigarette) is not suitable. Breakfast means BREAK-THE-FAST. Our bodies have fasted for some hours prior to breakfast - it needs a kick-start. Once we have eaten our metabolism will start working and continue for many hours after. If we miss breakfast our body thinks it is still fasting and will stay at a slow pace for the remainder of the day, which means kilojoules (energy) will burn slowly - not ideal for anyone wishing to lose weight.

- Research has shown that school children perform better if they have had breakfast. Children who don't are more likely to be tired and lack concentration mid morning. Also a higher level of industrial accidents occur in adults who miss breakfast.

- Missing breakfast, if anything, could be the reason why you may be hungry all day long or snack on high-fat, high-kilojoule snacks at morning tea time. Disaster on the waist line. Having a healthy breakfast may help you avoid this happening.

- Start the day with a good high-fibre cereal with skim milk, and fresh fruit. Another good choice is a skim milk smoothie; to make: place ice cubes in a blender, break them up, add cold skim milk, a little vanilla essence and a chilled banana or pineapple (any fruit you like), whiz together. YUM! And very filling.

- Have either wholemeal or multigrain toast with either baked beans, low-fat cheese and tomato or grilled tomato and mushrooms. These choices will help bulk you up and satisfy your hunger more easily until lunch time.

Lunch and Dinner

By the middle of the day your body has used up breakfast and will need refuelling. Always try, where possible, to include proteins with your lunch (low-fat cheese, salmon, lean chicken or lean meats, baked beans), and fill your sandwich high with salad as well. Most of us eat far more food than our bodies need especially at dinner time. The ideal dinner plate should have one third carbohydrates, such as rice, potato or pasta; one third salad or vegetables; and one third protein, such as meats, chicken, seafood, beans, tofu etc. Here are some tips:

- Firstly do not skip lunch - you are asking for disaster later in the day (bingeing).

- Wholemeal bread/rolls, lavash or pita breads, potato, rice or pasta are good carbohydrates, which will give you energy to get through the day.

- Deli meats are high in salt and fat so eat in moderation.

- Spread avocado on your sandwich instead of butter or margarine.

- If you have a big meal at lunch time, then don't have a large meal that night, instead reverse your meals so that dinner is a light meal. It's all about balancing your day.

- Use a small dinner plate.

- Use cooking sprays or baking paper instead of adding oil or fats to the pan. It is even better to grill, BBQ or bake. Forget deep frying anything.

- Use low-fat mayonnaise and dressings on your salads.

- Don't be tempted by the high-fat takeaway foods, they will only make you sluggish. Instead opt for healthy choices e.g. doner kebabs, hamburger (no fried onion or cheese), a stir fry or something from Subway.

- If eating at a restaurant avoid food that is fried. Ask for grilled fish, potato wedges or really big chips instead of the thinly cut variety (the larger chips have less fat), or better still have a jacket potato.

- Have tomato-based sauces instead of high-fat creamy ones. If a dish has a sauce or a salad has dressing, ask for it to be served on the side, then add as much or as little as you like.

- Avoid garlic bread or herb breads - too high in fat.

- Try to have alcohol in moderation. Drinking iced water or diet soft drink for some of the evening will help save on kilojoules.

- High-fat desserts are best kept for those special occasions (or share). You can't beat fresh fruit (or my recipes). Low-fat ice-creams, custards etc. are ideal to serve with dessert.

- Buy good quality meats - cut all the visible fat off and use only skinless chicken and choose the leanest mince you can find.

- Seafood is a great low-fat choice if cooked the right way. It's also really good for you.

- Choose low-fat recipes like in this cookbook. You will find the whole family will enjoy their food and it's good for them too.

- Eat slowly. It takes 20 minutes for your brain to tell your stomach when it is full.

Snacking

It may not be the meals but instead all the little snacks consumed throughout the day that are causing weight gain. Or are you an emotional eater, eating because of boredom, loneliness, needing comfort, eating for the sake of it or eating just out of habit. The 3-4 o'clock snack attack comes from when we were children rushing home from school and raiding the fridge. Ask yourself are you actually hungry or just eating from habit? Some people eat like a rabbit during the day and then become ravenous in the evening, bingeing on high-fat snacks. Such patterns can cause difficulty in controlling your weight. Snacking itself is not a problem, if we choose wisely, but be aware that all those bits and pieces can really add up. Plan your snacks and make time to shop wisely. Have healthy choices in the fridge/cupboard and you will avoid eating things you may regret later.

- Biscuits, cakes, doughnuts, pastry, ice-cream, chocolate and chips have very little nutritional value, are very high in fat and sugar, and have high kilojoules. Choose the healthier choices or think about omitting this type of food from your diet.

- A great snack is raisin toast or high fibre cereals with skim milk, and of course the best snack of all is fresh fruit. All these snack ideas are great when you get the munchies.

- If you crave sugar this could be a sign that your body may need protein, not a chocolate bar. Snack on low-fat yoghurts, light Fruche®, diet jellies, tinned fruit or skim milk smoothies (see breakfast tips). Low-fat ice-cream may help the sweet cravings too.

- Pretzels, low-fat popcorn, rice crackers, celery and carrots are great crunchy snacks.

- The best snack of all is fresh fruit, or vegetables with low-fat dips.

Shopping Smart

In my cookbooks all the recipes use ingredients that are in our cupboards and easily found in the supermarket.

- What does "LIGHT" mean on food labels? It could mean that it is light in flavour, colour, sugar, texture, fibre, salt or fat. Light may give the impression that a product is light in fat, so be careful e.g. Light Olive Oil means the oil is light in colour/flavour.

- "CHOLESTEROL FREE" is ideal for anyone concerned with cholesterol BUT this may not mean low fat. It can mean they have replaced the animal fat with vegetable fat, a healthier choice but of no advantage to slimmers. Read the nutritional information on each product first before you buy.

- "HIDDEN FATS" - Some crackers have 1g of fat per biscuit. Have your crackers but choose the healthy alternatives such as rice cakes or rice crackers or low-fat versions. Just be careful what you put on top.

- A product may be low in fat but high in kilojoules. To have a healthy balance go for both low fat and low kilojoules.

- I cannot find LITE or LO in the dictionary. The word "DIET" on a product means it is low in fat and sugar, perfect for anyone on a weight loss program.

- Don't grocery shop when hungry as you may choose things that you would not normally buy. Don't buy food that you cannot control - don't have food in the house that may tempt you. Make your house a safe zone, it really helps when those hunger pangs hit. I cannot stress how important this is.

The adjustable teaspoon and tablespoon can be purchased from my website:
www.symplytoogood.com.au
or Phone 07 5445 1250

Measuring Cups and Spoons

In every recipe a metric measuring cup and spoon were used. For example the tablespoon I have used, equals 15 grams. If you were using a metal tablespoon be aware that it could measure from 20 to 30 grams a spoon. I didn't use a tea cup. When I say 1 cup of flour, I have used a 250ml measuring cup as shown.

Testimonials

Many wonderful people have written letters, faxes and emails from all over the world. I feel blessed that so many people have taken the time out of their busy lives to write to me and I thank you all. I thought I would share some fantastic snippets from mail that I have received.

I wish to congratulate you! I have found your cookbook wonderful and use it constantly. Usually after purchasing a cookbook I find only a couple of recipes worth repeating, but in your cookbook they are ALL terrific.
Mrs Dorothy Helyar - Teesdale. VIC

I am writing to say that it was a very good day when by chance I watched "What's Cooking", you were the guest chef. What can I say about your book . . . easy instructions, recipes that look good and taste good, wonderful nutritional information. Your book is constantly by my side, I'm always referring to it for something, thankyou!
Jennifer Harman - Two Wells. SA

Thank you for producing a wonderfully researched and presented book of tasty, low-fat cooking, five weeks ago I bought your book and am delighted to say I've now lost 5 kgs.
Shiela Lee - Kenmore. QLD

CONGRATULATIONS on such a wonderful and impressive low-fat cookbook. With the help of your recipes I have lost 15 kilos and now realise that low-fat food and how it is prepared is what really is important in losing weight.
Vicki Rhodes - Allambie. NSW

I am writing to tell you of the success my husband and I have had using your cookbook. Just by following your easy healthy recipes and good advice I have lost 6 kilos and my husband has lost 10 kilos in just 5 months, even my cholesterol has gone down. It has been the best $9.95 I have ever spent.
Elizabeth Garnett - Narangba. QLD

There are many low-fat cookbooks out these days, but unfortunately they have recipes that a 'normal' family wouldn't eat. Thankyou! Thankyou, for putting out a low fat cookbook with 'normal' recipes.
Janet Wilson - Orange. NSW

My son was diagnosed with diabetes, I have found your recipes great! Thank you for writing/creating dishes that appeal to teenagers - but don't cost the earth in exotic ingredients.
Frances - Roma. QLD

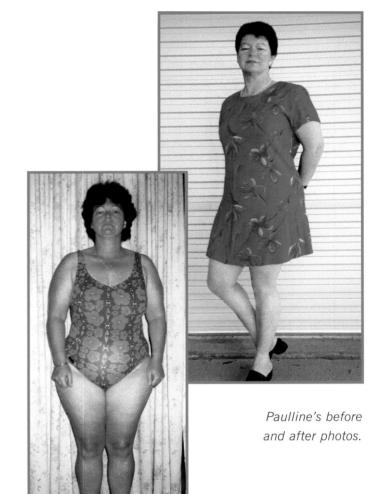

Paulline's before and after photos.

I have been on many diets over the years always culminating in the same result of weight on weight off. Since purchasing your book it seems so much easier, as a person who really enjoys her food I can honestly say that I no longer feel deprived. Over the last 2 years I have lost 30kg. Your book has been an inspiration in helping me to realise that food can still taste good, the Moist Fruit Cake is one of my favourites. All your recipes are so delicious and easy to make, my whole family eats and enjoys all the meals prepared out of your book. Thank you for the motivation and help that your book has given me to take the weight off and keep it off.
Paulline Beer - Stanthorpe. QLD

I am currently in my 2nd year of a Bachelor of Business, I work casually in a newsagency and have watched with amazement the success of your cookbook. The demand for your book is incredible, I have spoken to many happy customers - well done!
Emma Hansford - Fig Tree Pocket. QLD

Congratulations on a fantastic book. I have tried several of the recipes and found them very easy to make as well as tasty. I have a 3 year old and an 8 month old so easy meals are essential. In fact even my husband has been impressed with the flavour and taste. It is so hard being a mum at home not to pick at foods during the day, at least with your help now I can be picking at things which are low fat.

Joanna Taylor - Ringwood. VIC

I have no great cooking talents but find your recipes very easy and quick to make. Also they are good recipes for the whole family and contain ingredients which are easy to find in the supermarkets. My husband has to be on a low fat diet due to health problems which means your book is a blessing to us with the nutritional information. Your book is now affectionately know as "Our Bible".

Margaret Richards - Caloundra. QLD

Since buying your book I have not stopped using it, it is the best low fat book brought out so far. I love the Zucchini Slice and the Apple Strudel, I no longer feel deprived of food I love, thankyou.

Lesa Oliver - Redland Bay. QLD

Your book has been an absolute necessity in my kitchen. I recently attended one of your seminars and had to write to congratulate you on an outstanding presentation which I enjoyed, and now feel motivated to be the healthy person I deserve to be. Knowing you, too, have been overweight I felt you knew the pain and heart ache us fatties go through, seeing you now so slim has given me hope. If you can do it, so can I.

Cheryl Amies - Ballarat. VIC

I bought your book 6 weeks ago and since then have lost $6\frac{1}{2}$ kilos. I read the book from cover to cover, it was interesting to see the slight changes made to reduce the fat content. Thank you for helping me to attain a new lifestyle - eating plan. When friends ask what diet I am on this time, I stress that I am not on a diet - just a lifestyle change.

Helen Sigglekow - Maleny. QLD

I have lost 8 kilos since I started cooking your recipes, I am now more positive than a Duracell Battery.

Cathy Chapman - Reservoir. VIC

As a Dietitian in Private Practice I advise many clients on weight loss and how to improve their health through lower fat eating. I can wholeheartedly say I recommend your book as an important addition to the household recipe collection.

Sally Macqueen, Accredited Practising Dietitian - Brisbane. QLD

At our TOWN (Take Off Weight Naturally) Club meeting last week, a new member lost 2.8 kilos. I asked her to share with the group what her secret was, turns out everything she ate during the week came from your cookbook 'Symply Too Good To Be True'. In my opinion your cookbook must be considered required reading for anyone serious about long term weight control. Congratulations on an outstanding book.

Carol Shipard - Shepparton. VIC

Thanks to you, I've lost 3 kilos in 3 weeks!!!

Annette Digney - Craigieburn. VIC

Desley at 150 kilos and now on her way to her goal weight

With the help of your cookbook I have lost $9\frac{1}{2}$ stone (60 kilos). I feel so much healthier and have found my sugar levels, blood pressure and cholesterol are all back to normal again. Many thanks for your support, I spoke with you at a book signing you did at Ipswich recently, you are truly an inspiration to me and I will always remember how a total stranger with just a few words has given me the courage to keep going.

Desley Harwood - Gailes. QLD

Asparagus and Sweet Corn Soup

SERVES: 10

- 2 tablespoons (30g) Flora Light® margarine
- 1 cup onion diced
- 2 tablespoons plain flour
- 5 cups water
- 1 tablespoon salt-reduced chicken-style stock powder (Massel®)
- 2 x 340g cans asparagus tips and cuts drained
- 2 x 420g cans creamed corn
- 1 ½ cups frozen corn kernels
- 1 x 375ml can evaporated light milk
- pepper to taste

DIRECTIONS

Melt margarine in a boiler, add onion and cook 2 minutes. Add in flour and cook a further minute, slowly pour in water stirring continuously to avoid lumps. Add stock powder and all remaining ingredients except the milk. Bring to boil, simmer for 10 minutes with lid off, stirring occasionally to prevent mixture from sticking. Pour in milk, pepper to taste, bring back to boil then serve.

VARIATION: ADD 2 CUPS COOKED SKINLESS CHICKEN BREAST DICED.

Dietitian's Tip

Have this soup with a slice of multigrain bread for lunch or dinner. The meal is low in fat, high in fibre and the glycaemic index is low making it an ideal choice for people with diabetes.

Nutritional Information

PER SERVE		CHICKEN	ASP/CORN
FAT	TOTAL	4.1g	2.9g
	SATURATED	1.1g	0.8g
FIBRE		5.6g	5.6g
PROTEIN		13.8g	6.7g
CARBS		24.4g	24.4g
SUGAR		10.4g	10.4g
SODIUM		452mg	436mg
KILOJOULES		804 (cals 191)	639 (cals 152)
GI RATING		Low	Low

Potato & Leek Soup

SERVES: 8

- 3 cups leek sliced
- 2 tablespoons (30g) Flora Light® margarine
- 2 tablespoons plain flour
- 4 cups water
- 2 cups skim milk
- 6 cups (1kilo) potato peeled and diced
- 2 tablespoons salt-reduced chicken-style stock powder (Massel®)
- 1 x 375ml can evaporated light milk
- pepper to taste

DIRECTIONS

Cut leek lengthways into 2 pieces and wash well, cut into slices. Melt margarine in a boiler, place leek in pot and cook 1 minute, add flour and cook 1 minute. Slowly add in water and skim milk stirring continuously. Bring to boil then add diced potato and stock powder, simmer for 30 minutes with lid on, stir occasionally to prevent mixture from sticking. Pour in evaporated milk, bring back to boil, simmer 5 more minutes. Mash mixture until a fairly smooth consistency. Pepper to taste.

Dietitian's Tip

This is a great choice for people wanting a tasty soup with out the added sodium (salt). Ideal for those with high blood pressure.

Nutritional Information

PER SERVE		
FAT	TOTAL	3.0g
	SATURATED	0.9g
FIBRE		3.3g
PROTEIN		10.3g
CARBS		28.2g
SUGAR		10.8g
SODIUM		101mg
KILOJOULES		766 (cals 182)
GI RATING		Medium

Thai Soup

SERVES: 8

- 150g skinless chicken breast
- cooking spray
- 1 teaspoon crushed garlic (in jar)
- 1 teaspoon crushed ginger (in jar)
- ½ cup shallots sliced
- ½ cup red capsicum sliced
- ½ cup green capsicum sliced
- ½ x 227g can bamboo shoots drained sliced
- 1 cup mushrooms sliced
- 2 bok choy thinly sliced
- 2 tablespoons salt-reduced chicken-style stock powder (Massel®)
- 2 tablespoons fish sauce
- 2 tablespoons soy sauce 43% less salt
- 1½ litres water
- 1 cup hokkien noodles
- fresh chilli chopped (to taste, optional)
- ¼ cup fresh coriander leaves chopped
- 100g cooked peeled prawns

Dietitian's Tip

This soup is low in fat and kilojoules so can be included before a hearty meal without worrying about putting on weight.

DIRECTIONS

Cut chicken into small strips. Coat the base of a boiler or large saucepan with cooking spray. Brown chicken with garlic and ginger, add shallots, capsicum, bamboo shoots, mushrooms and bok choy, sauté 1 minute. Add stock powder, fish sauce and soy sauce, pour in water, bring to boil. Add hokkien noodles, chilli and coriander and simmer for 5 minutes. Add in cooked prawns just before serving.

Nutritional Information

PER SERVE		
FAT	TOTAL	0.7g
	SATURATED	0.1g
FIBRE		1.3g
PROTEIN		8.8g
CARBS		4.3g
SUGAR		1.1g
SODIUM		376mg
KILOJOULES		248 (cals 59)
GI RATING		Medium

Oysters Florentine

SERVES: 4

4 x 1 dozen natural oysters in shell

SAUCE
2 teaspoons (10g) Flora Light® margarine
½ teaspoon crushed garlic (in jar)
2 tablespoons plain flour
1½ cups skim milk
1 x 35g packet salt-reduced French onion soup (Continental®)
1 x 250g packet frozen spinach (defrosted)
1 cup 25% reduced-fat grated tasty cheese

DIRECTIONS

Melt margarine in a medium size saucepan, add garlic and cook for 30 seconds. Stir in flour and mix well using a whisk. Slowly add milk to saucepan, stirring continuously to avoid lumps. Add in dry soup mix and simmer 3 minutes. Stir in spinach and cook a further 2 minutes. Place oysters on a flat baking tray. Spoon sauce evenly over each oyster then top with cheese. Grill until golden brown.

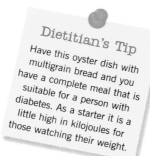

Dietitian's Tip
Have this oyster dish with multigrain bread and you have a complete meal that is suitable for a person with diabetes. As a starter it is a little high in kilojoules for those watching their weight.

Nutritional Information

PER SERVE		
FAT	TOTAL	9.6g
	SATURATED	5.0g
FIBRE		3.1g
PROTEIN		20.8g
CARBS		6.0g
SUGAR		5.3g
SODIUM		514mg
KILOJOULES		807 (cals 192)
GI RATING		Too low in carbs to score a rating

Sausage Rolls

MAKES: 4 LARGE OR 12 SMALL

½ cup dried breadcrumbs
½ cup skim milk
200g very lean beef mince
100g sausage mince
½ small onion finely diced
½ teaspoon mixed herbs
pepper to taste
8 sheets filo pastry
cooking spray

Dietitian's Tip
This recipe will provide you with a low fat starter or meal, depending on the size of the roll. This is low in saturated fat thus ideal for those with heart disease or diabetes.

DIRECTIONS

Preheat oven 200ºC fan forced.

Mix breadcrumbs and milk in a small bowl, leave for 2 minutes. In a medium size mixing bowl combine all ingredients except filo pastry, using your hands mix the ingredients together well. Layer all sheets of filo pastry on top of each other spraying with cooking spray between each layer. Cut in half. Divide sausage mix in half and roll one half into a long sausage shape that will fit onto cut pastry sheets. Tightly but gently roll the sheets away from you (like a Swiss roll). Repeat this again with remaining ingredients. For large sausage rolls cut each roll in half (4 sausage rolls). For small sausage rolls cut each roll into 6 pieces (12 sausage rolls). Place on a flat baking tray that has been coated with cooking spray. Bake approximately 20 minutes.

Nutritional Information

PER ROLL		SMALL	LARGE
FAT	TOTAL	3.4g	10.2g
	SATURATED	1.5g	4.4g
FIBRE		0.5g	1.6g
PROTEIN		6.3g	18.9g
CARBS		8.5g	25.4g
SUGAR		1.0g	3.1g
SODIUM		161mg	484mg
KILOJOULES		376 (cals 90)	1127 (cals 268)
GI RATING		Medium	Medium

Fettuccine Carbonara

SERVES: 6

cooking spray

1 teaspoon crushed garlic (in jar)

1 small onion diced

1 cup 97% fat-free ham diced (Hans®)

3 cups mushrooms sliced

1 tablespoon (15g) Flora Light® margarine

2 tablespoons plain flour

1 x 375ml can evaporated light milk

¾ cup skim milk

2 sachets cream of mushroom cup-a-soup (Continental®)

1 teaspoon salt-reduced vegetable stock powder (Massel®)

2 tablespoons grated parmesan cheese

pepper to taste

300g dry fettuccine pasta

Dietitian's Tip
97% fat free ham can be used in all recipes to lower the amount of saturated fat and make it suitable for people with diabetes.

DIRECTIONS

Coat a large non-stick saucepan with cooking spray. Sauté garlic and onion for 2 minutes, toss in ham and cook 2 minutes. Add sliced mushrooms and cook a further 2-3 minutes. Remove from pan and set to one side. In same saucepan melt margarine, add flour, mixing well. Slowly add in evaporated milk and then skim milk, mixing continually until smooth. Stir in dry soup mix, stock powder and parmesan cheese. Return mushroom mixture to pot, combine well, add pepper to taste. Fill a large saucepan ¾ full with water: Bring to boil, add pasta, bring back to boil then simmer stirring occasionally to keep pasta separated. Cook 10 minutes or until pasta is cooked, drain, divide into 6 serves. Pour sauce over pasta and serve.

Nutritional Information

PER SERVE			CARBS	47.7g
FAT	TOTAL	4.3g	SUGAR	9.9g
	SATURATED	1.8g	SODIUM	366mg
FIBRE		3.8g	KILOJOULES	1210 (cals 288)
PROTEIN		17.5g	GI RATING	Low

Stinky Bread

SERVES: 4

2 teaspoons (10g) Flora Light® margarine

4 slices multigrain bread

4 teaspoons grated parmesan cheese

paprika

DIRECTIONS

Spread margarine over bread slices. Sprinkle 1 teaspoon of cheese over top of each slice of bread, lightly shake a little paprika over top. Place under grill, bread is ready when golden brown. No need to cook other side.

Nutritional Information

PER SERVE			CARBS	11.1g
FAT	TOTAL	2.8g	SUGAR	0.6g
	SATURATED	0.8g	SODIUM	178mg
FIBRE		1.2g	KILOJOULES	348 (cals 83)
PROTEIN		3.4g	GI RATING	Low

Macaroni Cheese

SERVES: 4

2 cups raw macaroni noodles

2 cups skim milk

2 sachets 4 cheese sauce (Continental®)

½ cup 25% reduced-fat grated tasty cheese

1 tablespoon grated parmesan cheese

pepper to taste

DIRECTIONS

Cook pasta as directed on packet. Rinse well and leave to one side. Using the same saucepan bring milk to boil, add sauce sachets and whisk together. Add in grated cheese, parmesan cheese, pepper to taste. Bring back to boil stirring continuously. Place noodles into sauce and fold until pasta is well coated.

VARIATION: ADD ½ CUP OF FRESH TOMATO DICED.

Dietitian's Tip

This dish may be too high in carbohydrate for some people with diabetes particularly if they also intend to have bread or a high carbohydrate dessert.

Nutritional Information

PER SERVE		
FAT	TOTAL	5.4g
	SATURATED	3.0g
FIBRE		3.1g
PROTEIN		19.0g
CARBS		52.0g
SUGAR		6.8g
SODIUM		471mg
KILOJOULES		1405 (cals 335)
GI RATING		Low

Quiche Lorraine

SERVES: 6

PASTRY

¾ cup self-raising flour

1 cup plain flour

2 tablespoons (30g) Flora Light® margarine

¼ cup skim milk

1 egg white

flour to roll pastry

cooking spray

FILLING

2 whole eggs

2 egg whites

1 x 375ml can evaporated light milk

½ cup shallots chopped

1 cup 97% fat-free ham diced (Hans®)

½ cup 25% reduced-fat grated tasty cheese

1 tablespoon grated parmesan cheese

pepper to taste

Dietitian's Tip

With a green salad this is a great meal that is low in fat and high in vitamins and minerals such as calcium and iron. Ideal for people with diabetes.

DIRECTIONS

Preheat oven 180°C fan forced.

To make pastry: Sift both flours together in a large mixing bowl. Melt margarine then stir into milk. Beat egg white into milk mixture using a fork until blended. Pour milk mixture into flour and gently fold together. Place pastry on a well-floured bench, roll out to fit a round pie dish (23cm). Place rolled pastry over base of pie dish that has been coated with cooking spray. Using a sharp knife trim around any hanging edges to neaten. Leave to one side.

To make filling: In a large bowl beat whole eggs and egg whites well, add milk and beat until well combined. Add all other ingredients and mix together well. Pour into prepared pie dish. Bake 35-40 minutes or until golden brown and cooked in centre.

Nutritional Information

PER SERVE		
FAT	TOTAL	8.7g
	SATURATED	3.6g
FIBRE		1.7g
PROTEIN		19.7g
CARBS		38.3g
SUGAR		8.4g
SODIUM		574mg
KILOJOULES		1248 (cals 297)
GI RATING		Medium

Chicken and Corn Pie

SERVES: 6

½ cup raw Basmati rice

BASE

1 onion diced

cooking spray

1 teaspoon each cumin, turmeric, coriander

¼ teaspoon chilli powder (or to taste)

½ cup dried breadcrumbs

1 egg

1 tablespoon skim milk

TOPPING

2 whole eggs

3 egg whites

½ cup skim milk

2 cups (200g) zucchini grated

1 x 310g can creamed corn

1 cup frozen corn kernels

1 cup (140g) skinless cooked chicken breast shredded

½ cup 25% reduced-fat grated tasty cheese

⅓ cup fresh parsley chopped

½ teaspoon tarragon

1 teaspoon salt-reduced chicken-style stock powder (Massel®)

pepper to taste

¼ cup 25% reduced-fat grated tasty cheese

Dietitian's Tip

Unlike many pies this is low in saturated fat and contains lean meats making it suitable for people with diabetes.

DIRECTIONS

Cook rice, drain well. Preheat oven 200°C fan forced.

To make base: Sauté onion for 2-3 minutes in a non-stick frypan that has been coated with cooking spray. Add cumin, turmeric, coriander and chilli powder to pan and cook a further 1 minute. Tip onion mix into a medium size mixing bowl, add in cooked rice and breadcrumbs, and mix well. Beat egg with milk then pour into rice mixture, combine ingredients together well. Coat a pie dish (23cm) with cooking spray then press rice mixture into dish evenly

To make topping: In a large mixing bowl beat eggs, egg whites and milk together. Add remaining ingredients except ¼ cup (25g) grated cheese (to put on top of pie), mix all ingredients together well. Pour mixture over rice base, sprinkle remaining cheese over top and bake uncovered for 50-60 minutes or until set and brown on top. Let stand for 10-15 minutes before serving.

Serve hot or cold, a salad goes very nicely with the pie. (Can be made the day before)

VARIATIONS: REPLACE CHICKEN WITH 1 CUP OF 97% FAT-FREE HAM (HANS®) DICED OR REPLACE CHICKEN WITH 1 CUP DRAINED TUNA IN BRINE.

Nutritional Information

PER SERVE		CHICKEN	HAM	TUNA
FAT	TOTAL	6.8g	6.1g	7.3g
	SATURATED	2.5g	2.4g	2.8g
FIBRE		4.2g	4.2g	3.3g
PROTEIN		19.4g	15.5g	26.4g
CARBS		36.0g	36.2g	30.2g
SUGAR		6.3g	6.4g	5.6g
SODIUM		363mg	568mg	492mg
KILOJOULES		1184 (cals 282)	1036 (cals 247)	1223 (cals 291)
GI RATING		Low	Low	Low

Vegetables and Salads

Symslaw

SERVES: 12

¼ cup (20g) pine nuts
1 teaspoon curry powder (or to taste)
½ cup 97% fat-free mayonnaise
¼ cabbage thinly shredded
1 cup red capsicum diced
1 small onion finely diced
1 cup carrot grated
1 cup celery sliced
1 cup mushrooms sliced
1 small apple diced (skin on)
⅓ cup sultanas
pepper to taste

Dietitian's Tip

This recipe provides loads of fibre, vitamins and minerals as well as essential fatty acids. Include this into your eating plan to protect you against many cancers.

DIRECTIONS

Spread pine nuts on a baking tray, place under grill until browned on both sides (be careful as they burn quickly), leave to cool. Stir curry powder into mayonnaise. In a large mixing bowl place all ingredients and mix together well. Refrigerate until required.

Nutritional Information

PER SERVE				
FAT	TOTAL	1.5g	CARBS	11.4g
	SATURATED	0.1g	SUGAR	10.3g
			SODIUM	122mg
FIBRE		2.7g	KILOJOULES	280 (cals 67)
PROTEIN		1.7g	GI RATING	Medium

Tabouli

SERVES: 10

¾ cup dried (bourghul) cracked wheat
3 cups water
2 tomatoes
1½ cups fresh parsley (about 1 bunch)
½ cup mint leaves
3 tablespoons lemon juice
1 cup onion chopped
1 teaspoon crushed garlic (in jar)
pepper to taste

Dietitian's Tip

This dish is low in kilojoules and has abundant vitamins and minerals. The fact that it has a low glycaemic index adds to its appeal for people with diabetes.

DIRECTIONS

In a medium size mixing bowl place cracked wheat and water. Allow to stand for 1 hour, stir occasionally. Drain well, place into a large mixing bowl. Cut tomatoes in ½ and using a dessertspoon scoop out inside (not required), now cut tomato skin into small dices, add to bowl. Chop parsley and mint, add to bowl with lemon juice, onion and garlic. Pepper to taste, mix well. Refrigerate.

Nutritional Information

PER SERVE				
FAT	TOTAL	0.3g	CARBS	8.9g
	SATURATED	0g	SUGAR	1.0g
			SODIUM	49mg
FIBRE		3.1g	KILOJOULES	200 (cals 48)
PROTEIN		2.0g	GI RATING	Low

Potato Salad

SERVES: 8

1 kilo washed new potatoes
½ cup shallots sliced
1 tablespoon mint finely chopped
⅓ cup 97% fat-free mayonnaise
pepper to taste

DIRECTIONS

Leaving skin on, cut potatoes in ½ then into cubes. Cook potatoes in microwave with a little water for 12-15 minutes or until potato is just cooked. Drain, run cold water over potato for a minute. Place potato in a large mixing bowl with all other ingredients. Gently fold ingredients together, being careful not to break up potato. Pepper to taste, refrigerate.

Dietitian's Tip

This low fat potato salad can be included into the eating plan of people with diabetes or heart disease.

Nutritional Information

PER SERVE		
FAT	TOTAL	0.4g
	SATURATED	0.1g
FIBRE		1.5g
PROTEIN		3.5g
CARBS		20.9g
SUGAR		4.3g
SODIUM		121mg
KILOJOULES		435 (cals 104)
GI RATING		High

Vegetable Risotto

SERVES: 6

2 teaspoons (10g) Flora Light® margarine

1 onion finely diced

1 teaspoon crushed garlic (in jar)

2 cups raw arborio rice

3 cups salt-reduced vegetable stock liquid (Campbells®)

2 teaspoons salt-reduced vegetable stock powder (Massel®)

⅓ cup dry white wine

3 cups water

2 cups mushrooms sliced

1 cup fresh green beans sliced

1 cup frozen corn kernels

1 cup red capsicum diced

3 tablespoons grated parmesan cheese

pepper to taste

Dietitian's Tip
A great dish for vegetarians and active people with diabetes as it has a high quantity of high glycaemic index aborio rice.

DIRECTIONS

You must cook this recipe in a large non-stick saucepan.

Melt margarine, add onion and garlic, cook 2 minutes. Add in rice and cook for 3 minutes, stirring frequently. Add 2 cups of stock liquid and all stock powder, bring to boil, simmer stirring frequently until liquid has been absorbed by rice. Add in wine, once absorbed pour in 1 cup of stock liquid and 1 cup water, bring back to boil. Add mushrooms, beans, corn and capsicum, reduce to a simmer stirring frequently until water is absorbed. Add final 2 cups of water. When almost all liquid has been absorbed (rice should be cooked by this stage) stir in parmesan cheese, pepper to taste. Serve.

*Note: Risotto when cooked should have a moist consistency.

Nutritional Information

PER SERVE			CARBS	63.9g
FAT	TOTAL	3.0g	SUGAR	4.3g
	SATURATED	1.2g	SODIUM	387mg
FIBRE		4.2g	KILOJOULES	1405 (cals 335)
PROTEIN		10.7g	GI RATING	Medium

Sweet Potato Chips

SERVES: 6

1 kilo sweet potato
cooking spray

DIRECTIONS

Preheat oven 220ºC fan forced.

Peel and cut sweet potatoes into slices then into chip shapes. Coat surface of a flat baking tray generously with cooking spray. Place chips on tray and generously coat with cooking spray. Bake on top rack of oven 25-30 minutes or until golden brown, turning once.

Dietitian's Tip
Sweet potato has a low glycaemic index and by using this recipe the chips are also low in fat. This makes them ideal for people with diabetes.

Nutritional Information

PER SERVE			CARBS	27.8g
FAT	TOTAL	0.2g	SUGAR	7.8g
	SATURATED	0g	SODIUM	20mg
FIBRE		3.2g	KILOJOULES	518 (cals 123)
PROTEIN		2.5g	GI RATING	Low

Pizza Potato Bake

SERVES: 8

1 kilo peeled potatoes
1 cup capsicum diced
1 cup 97% fat-free ham (Hans®) diced
1 cup shallots sliced or onion diced
½ cup fresh tomato diced
¾ cup 25% reduced-fat grated tasty cheese
2 tablespoons grated parmesan cheese
1 teaspoon crushed garlic (in jar)
½ teaspoon dried basil
cooking spray
1 x 415g can no added salt chopped tomato
1 cup water

Dietitian's Tip
A tasty low fat, low sodium vegetable accompaniment to a meal. Include this in your eating plan to help prevent chronic diseases such as diabetes, heart disease and cancer.

DIRECTIONS

Preheat oven 220ºC fan forced.

Thinly slice peeled potatoes and microwave in a little water for 12-15 minutes or until potato is just cooked. Drain, run cold water over potato to cool (be careful not to break up potato). In a large mixing bowl place all other ingredients except the chopped tomato and water. In a large lasagne dish that has been coated with cooking spray place ½ of the potato slices, sprinkle half the pizza mix over potato, spread remaining potato over top. In a small bowl mix canned tomatoes and water together, pour over top of potato, top with remaining pizza mix. Cover with foil (spray foil with cooking spray to avoid food sticking), bake for 1 hour, remove foil and cook a further 15 minutes or until top has browned.

VARIATION: TO MAKE VEGETARIAN OMIT HAM AND REPLACE WITH 1½ CUPS MUSHROOMS DICED.

Potato Bake

SERVES: 8

1 kilo potatoes peeled
cooking spray
1 cup 25% reduced-fat grated tasty cheese
4 tablespoons grated parmesan cheese
1½ cups skim milk
2 x 30g sachets 4 cheese sauce (Continental®)

DIRECTIONS

Preheat oven 200ºC fan forced.

Peel potatoes and slice thinly. Place ½ the potato slices in a lasagne dish that has been coated with cooking spray. Sprinkle ½ the grated cheese and ½ the parmesan cheese over potatoes, top with remaining potatoes. In a small saucepan bring milk to boil, add sauce sachets and whisk together. Pour over potato. Now sprinkle over the remaining parmesan cheese and grated cheese. Cover with foil (spray foil with cooking spray to avoid food sticking). Bake for 1 hour, remove foil and cook a further 10-15 minutes or until potato is cooked.

Dietitian's Tip
A high calcium, low fat recipe that is tasty and will help to build strong bones.

Nutritional Information

PER SERVE		PIZZA	VEGETARIAN
FAT	TOTAL	3.4g	3.1g
	SATURATED	1.9g	1.8g
FIBRE		2.9g	3.3g
PROTEIN		9.4g	7.8g
CARBS		19.9g	20.0g
SUGAR		3.4g	3.4g
SODIUM		268mg	104mg
KILOJOULES		584 (cals 139)	593 (cals 141)
GI RATING		High	High

Nutritional Information

PER SERVE		
FAT	TOTAL	4.5g
	SATURATED	2.8g
FIBRE		2.0g
PROTEIN		9.8g
CARBS		19.7g
SUGAR		3.2g
SODIUM		198mg
KILOJOULES		671 (cals 160)
GI RATING		High

Asparagus and Ham Slice

SERVES: 6

2 whole eggs

3 egg whites

1 x 410g can asparagus tips and cuts drained

¾ cup (75g) 97% fat-free ham (Hans®) diced

1 cup red capsicum diced

1 cup frozen corn kernels

1 onion diced

¾ cup self-raising flour

pepper to taste

1 cup 25% reduced-fat grated tasty cheese

cooking spray

Dietitian's Tip
This recipe uses fat reduced cheese and low-fat ham. A great way to lower saturated fat and kilojoules making it suitable for people with diabetes.

DIRECTIONS

Preheat oven 180°C fan forced.

In a large mixing bowl beat eggs and egg whites together for 2 minutes, add all other ingredients except cheese, mix together. Fold ½ the cheese into mixture. Coat a quiche dish with cooking spray, spoon mixture into dish then level mixture with back of spoon, sprinkle remaining cheese on top. Bake 30-35 minutes or until golden brown and cooked through.

VARIATIONS: REPLACE HAM WITH CELERY DICED OR CARROT GRATED FOR VEGETARIAN SLICE OR REPLACE HAM WITH COOKED SKINLESS CHICKEN BREAST DICED.

Nutritional Information

PER SERVE		HAM	VEGETARIAN	CHICKEN
FAT	TOTAL	6.8g	6.5g	8.1g
	SATURATED	3.5g	3.3g	3.8g
FIBRE		3.3g	3.8g	3.3g
PROTEIN		14.7g	12.8g	18.6g
CARBS		18.1g	18.7g	17.9g
SUGAR		2.8g	3.4g	2.7g
SODIUM		625mg	467mg	479mg
KILOJOULES		768 (cals 183)	779 (cals 185)	925 (cals 220)
GI RATING		Medium	Medium	Medium

Bean Surprise

SERVES: 2

1 x 425g can salt-reduced baked beans

½ cup zucchini grated

½ cup red capsicum diced

¾ cup mushrooms diced

⅓ cup celery diced

¼ cup onion diced

⅓ cup tomato diced

DIRECTIONS

Place all ingredients into a microwave-safe dish that has a lid, cook with lid on for 5 minutes on HIGH. Serve on toast or over a jacket potato.

Dietitian's Tip
A high fibre, low glycaemic index vegetarian recipe that would be ideal for people aiming to lose weight who have diabetes.

Nutritional Information

PER SERVE		
FAT	TOTAL	1.4g
	SATURATED	0.2g
FIBRE		12.7g
PROTEIN		12.7g
CARBS		28.1g
SUGAR		13.6g
SODIUM		184mg
KILOJOULES		739 (cals 176)
GI RATING		Low

Thai Curry Vegetables

SERVES: 4 LARGE OR 8 SIDE DISH

cooking spray

1 teaspoon ginger (in jar)

1 teaspoon garlic (in jar)

1 cup onion sliced

2 teaspoons massaman curry paste (in jar)

2½ cups water

2 teaspoons salt-reduced vegetable stock powder (Massel®)

3 cups new potatoes diced (skin on)

2 cups pumpkin diced

1 cup cauliflower small florets

1 cup broccoli small florets

1 cup yellow squash cut into quarters

1 cup cabbage thickly sliced

1 cup green beans sliced

3 tablespoons cornflour

1 x 375ml can evaporated light milk

1 teaspoon imitation coconut essence

DIRECTIONS

In a boiler that has been coated with cooking spray cook ginger and garlic for 1 minute, add onion and massaman curry paste. Add in water and stock powder, toss in all vegetables and stir well. Bring to boil, simmer 15 minutes with lid on. Combine cornflour with milk and coconut essence, add to pot and bring back to boil. Be careful not to break up potato and pumpkin when stirring. Cook a further 5 minutes or until potato is cooked. Serve with couscous, rice, noodles or as a side dish to go with meat/chicken.

Dietitian's Tip

A clever use of coconut essence and evaporated milk to give the creamy coconut flavour without the fat. This is a great choice for vegetarians who have diabetes.

Nutritional Information

PER SERVE		LARGE	SIDE DISH
FAT	TOTAL	2.7g	1.3g
	SATURATED	1.2g	0.6g
FIBRE		7.5g	3.7g
PROTEIN		16.2g	8.1g
CARBS		39.0g	19.5g
SUGAR		18.5g	9.3g
SODIUM		163mg	81mg
KILOJOULES		1041 (cals 248)	520 (cals 124)
GI RATING		Medium	Medium

Seafood

Lemon Fish

SERVES: 4

- 1 tablespoon (15g) Flora Light® margarine
- ¼ teaspoon crushed garlic (in jar)
- 1 tablespoon plain flour
- ½ cup skim milk
- ½ teaspoon chicken stock powder
- 1 tablespoon white wine
- 2 tablespoons fresh lemon juice
- 1 teaspoon fresh coriander chopped
- pepper to taste
- 4 x 125g fish fillets
- cooking spray

Dietitian's Tip
The National Heart Foundation recommends that we all have three serves of fish per week so we have sufficient essential fatty acids for our heart health.

DIRECTIONS

In a non-stick saucepan melt margarine with garlic, add flour and combine. Slowly add in milk, using a whisk to avoid lumps, until boiling. Add stock powder, wine, lemon juice, coriander, pepper to taste. Cook fish fillets in a non-stick frypan that has been generously coated with cooking spray, turning once. Pour sauce over fillets and serve.

VARIATIONS: REPLACE FISH FILLETS WITH SKINLESS CHICKEN BREASTS OR 400g GREEN PRAWNS.

Nutritional Information

PER SERVE		FISH	CHICKEN	PRAWN
FAT	TOTAL	2.9g	4.9g	2.6g
	SATURATED	0.7g	1.2g	0.5g
FIBRE		0.2g	0.2g	0.2g
PROTEIN		26.3g	29.8g	22.0g
CARBS		3.5g	3.5g	3.5g
SUGAR		1.8g	1.8g	1.8g
SODIUM		209mg	191mg	472mg
KILOJOULES		624 (cals 149)	758 (cals 180)	543 (cals 129)
GI RATING			Too low in carbs to score a rating	

Fish Delish

SERVES: 4

- cooking spray
- 4 x 125g fish fillets
- 8 teaspoons traditional pesto (in jar)
- ¾ cup 25% reduced-fat grated tasty cheese

DIRECTIONS

Cook fish fillets in a non-stick frypan that has been generously coated with cooking spray, turning once. Once cooked, place fish on a flat baking tray that has been coated with cooking spray. Spread 2 teaspoons of pesto sauce over each piece of fish, top with cheese. Place tray under grill and cook until cheese has melted and is golden brown. Using an egg lifter slide under fish and serve.

VARIATIONS: REPLACE FISH FILLETS WITH SKINLESS CHICKEN BREAST OR LEAN RUMP STEAK.

Dietitian's Tip
This recipe may have more total fat than other recipes but the saturated fats are low making the recipe suitable for people with diabetes.

Nutritional Information

PER SERVE		FISH	CHICKEN	RUMP
FAT	TOTAL	10.1g	12.1g	12.5g
	SATURATED	4.3g	5.0g	5.6g
FIBRE		0.2g	0.2g	0.2g
PROTEIN		29.2g	35.6g	36.6g
CARBS		0.1g	0.1g	0.1g
SUGAR		0.1g	0.1g	0.1g
SODIUM		368mg	325mg	319mg
KILOJOULES		872 (cals 208)	1054 (cals 251)	1085 (cals 258)
GI RATING			Too low in carbs to score a rating	

Curried Prawns

Dietitian's Tip
Prawns are an occasional food for most of us and this recipe may be a little higher in sodium than recommended for people with diabetes - have it occasionally and use the meat options regularly.

SERVES: 4

cooking spray

400g raw green prawn meat

1 teaspoon crushed garlic (in jar)

1 teaspoon turmeric

1 teaspoon dried coriander

1 teaspoon cumin

1 teaspoon garam masala

¼ teaspoon chilli powder (to taste)

2 teaspoons salt-reduced chicken-style stock powder (Massel®)

½ cup red capsicum sliced

½ cup green capsicum sliced

1 cup onion sliced

1 tablespoon cornflour

1 teaspoon imitation coconut essence

1 x 375ml can evaporated light milk

pepper to taste

DIRECTIONS

In a non-stick frypan that has been generously coated with cooking spray, toss prawns for 3 minutes, add garlic and toss for 2 minutes. Add turmeric, coriander, cumin, garam masala, chilli powder and stock powder into pan, toss for 1 minute. Add capsicum and onion, cook 2 minutes. Combine cornflour, essence and milk together then add to pan stirring continuously until boiled, cook a few minutes more, pepper to taste. Serve with rice or noodles.

VARIATIONS: REPLACE PRAWNS WITH 500g SKINLESS CHICKEN BREAST SLICED OR 500g LEAN RUMP SLICED OR 500g LEAN LAMB LEG STEAK SLICED.

Nutritional Information

PER SERVE	PRAWN	CHICKEN	RUMP	LAMB
FAT TOTAL	2.5g	4.5g	4.9g	4.4g
SATURATED	1.2g	1.8g	2.4g	2.3g
FIBRE	0.8g	0.8g	0.8g	0.8g
PROTEIN	32.5g	37.1g	38.1g	37.3g
CARBS	14.8g	14.8g	14.8g	14.8g
SUGAR	13.0g	13.0g	13.0g	13.0g
SODIUM	581mg	164mg	158mg	176mg
KILOJOULES	896 (cals 213)	1046 (cals 249)	1077 (cals 256)	1046 (cals 249)
GI RATING	Low	Low	Low	Low

Fish Florentine

SERVES: 6

2 teaspoons (10g) Flora Light® margarine

½ teaspoon crushed garlic (in jar)

2 tablespoons plain flour

1½ cups skim milk

1 x 40g packet salt-reduced French onion soup mix

1 x 250g packet frozen spinach (defrosted)

6 x 120g boneless fish fillets

cooking spray

1 cup 25% reduced-fat grated tasty cheese

DIRECTIONS

Melt margarine in a medium size saucepan, add garlic and cook for 30 seconds. Stir in flour and mix well using a whisk. Slowly add milk, stirring continuously to avoid lumps. Add in dry soup mix and simmer 3 minutes. Stir in spinach, cook a further 2 minutes. Cook fish fillets in a non-stick fry pan that has been generously coated with cooking spray, turning once. Once cooked, place fish on a flat baking tray that has been coated with cooking spray, spoon sauce over each piece. Sprinkle cheese on top of sauce. Place under a grill until cheese has melted and is golden brown. Using an egg lifter slide under fish and place on a plate.

VARIATIONS: REPLACE FISH WITH SKINLESS CHICKEN BREASTS, LEAN RUMP STEAKS OR PORK BUTTERFLY STEAKS.

Dietitian's Tip
Fish is an excellent source of protein, is low in fat and contains essential fats this makes it great food for the brain.

Nutritional Information

PER SERVE	FISH	CHICKEN	RUMP	PORK
FAT TOTAL	6.4g	8.3g	8.6g	6.5g
SATURATED	3.3g	3.7g	4.3g	3.4g
FIBRE	2.2g	2.2g	2.2g	2.2g
PROTEIN	33.1g	36.5g	37.5g	37.6g
CARBS	5.8g	5.8g	5.8g	5.8g
SUGAR	3.5g	3.5g	3.5g	3.5g
SODIUM	302mg	284mg	278mg	287mg
KILOJOULES	893 (cals 213)	1022 (cals 243)	1052 (cals 250)	974 (cals 232)
GI RATING	Low	Low	Low	Low

Seafood Pie

SERVES: 4

cooking spray
1 teaspoon crushed garlic
150g raw green prawn meat
125g sea scallops
550g firm boneless fish fillets
(cut into bite-size pieces)
2 tablespoons brandy
¼ cup white wine
2 tablespoons lemon juice
1 tablespoon (15g) Flora Light® margarine
3 tablespoons plain flour
¼ cup skim milk
½ cup shallots sliced
1 tablespoon fresh parsley chopped
pepper to taste
7 sheets filo pastry

Dietitian's Tip
Generally pies are high in fat and often saturated fat. However in this recipe Annette cleverly uses filo pastry and a low-fat filling to make it suitable for people with diabetes.

DIRECTIONS

Coat a non-stick saucepan with cooking spray, cook garlic, prawns and scallops together for 2 minutes. Add fish, brandy, wine and lemon juice, cook a few more minutes. Place seafood and the liquid from pan into a medium size mixing bowl, leave to one side. Return pot to heat, melt margarine, stir in flour. Slowly add milk using a whisk to avoid lumps. Add shallots and parsley, cook 1 minute, return seafood and liquid to pot, bring to boil, pepper to taste. Simmer for a few minutes until sauce is thick. Set aside to cool.

Preheat oven 200°C fan forced.

Spray pie dish (20cm) with cooking spray. Cut filo sheets in half (use 8 for base, 6 for top). Layer pie dish with 8 x ½ cut sheets, in a rotating fashion, spraying with cooking spray between each sheet. Spread seafood mixture on top of pastry sheets. Place remaining filo sheets by layering over top of filling in a rotating fashion. Crinkle edges together, spray with cooking spray. Bake 30-35 minutes or until golden brown. Serve immediately as pastry will soften when left. To crisp again, either place back in oven or under grill.

Nutritional Information

PER SERVE				
FAT	TOTAL	3.9g	CARBS	19.6g
	SATURATED	0.9g	SUGAR	1.8g
FIBRE		0.9g	SODIUM	488mg
PROTEIN		42.5g	KILOJOULES	1311 (cals 312)
			GI RATING	Medium

Thai Fish Cakes

MAKES: 12

500g boneless fish fillets
3 tablespoons cornflour
2 teaspoons fish sauce
2 egg whites
½ cup coriander leaves
½ cup shallots chopped
1 cup dried breadcrumbs
4 teaspoons red curry paste
2 teaspoons sweet chilli sauce
plain flour for coating
cooking spray

Dietitian's Tip
As these cakes are not deep fried they are lower in fat than most and are ideal for everyone including people with diabetes watching their weight.

DIRECTIONS

Place fish pieces into a food processor and process a few minutes. Add all remaining ingredients and process until a reasonably smooth consistency is reached. Roll into 12 cakes then lightly coat in plain flour. Generously spray a non-stick frypan with cooking spray, when hot fry fish cakes until cooked on both sides. Serve with sweet chilli sauce (extra).

Nutritional Information

PER CAKE				
FAT	TOTAL	1.2g	CARBS	6.8g
	SATURATED	0.2g	SUGAR	0.5g
FIBRE		0.5g	SODIUM	299mg
PROTEIN		10.0g	KILOJOULES	330 (cals 79)
			GI RATING	High

Chicken

Chicken and Cashew Stir Fry

SERVES: 6

cooking spray

1 teaspoon crushed garlic (in jar)

¼ cup (30g) raw cashews

500g skinless chicken breast fillets sliced

½ cup onion sliced

½ small fresh red chilli sliced (optional)

½ cup green capsicum strips

½ cup red capsicum strips

16 snow peas cut in half

½ cup carrots cut in half then in thin slices

1 dessertspoon cornflour

1¼ cups water

1 teaspoon reduced-salt chicken-style stock powder (Massel®)

2 teaspoons fish sauce

2 teaspoons oyster sauce

2 teaspoons soy sauce 43% less salt

1 pinch of sugar

1 pinch of pepper

½ cup shallots

Dietitian's Tip

Cashew nuts add variety to stir fry dishes and are a great source of unsaturated fat making this recipe a healthy heart choice.

DIRECTIONS

Heat wok or large non-stick frypan and coat with cooking spray. Cook garlic and cashews for 1 minute, add chicken and toss until cooked, put chicken mixture into a bowl and leave to one side. Now add the onion, chilli, capsicum, snow peas and carrots, stir 3-5 minutes. Add cornflour to water and mix until blended; pour into pan with stock powder, sauces, sugar, pepper and shallots, stir them well; cook a couple of minutes more then serve with Basmati rice or noodles.

Nutritional Information

PER SERVE		WITH CASHEWS	WITHOUT CASHEWS
FAT	TOTAL	6.8g	3.1g
	SATURATED	1.4g	0.8g
FIBRE		2.1g	1.7g
PROTEIN		31.3g	30.0g
CARBS		7.2g	5.9g
SUGAR		4.8g	4.4g
SODIUM		537mg	536mg
KILOJOULES		903 (cals 215)	724 (cals 172)
GI RATING		Too low in carbs to score a rating	

Chicken Stroganoff

SERVES: 4

cooking spray

1 teaspoon crushed garlic (in jar)

600g skinless chicken breast (cut into strips)

1 cup onion sliced

3 cups mushrooms sliced

2 gherkins (finely chopped)

2 teaspoons salt-reduced chicken-style stock powder (Massel®)

2 tablespoons no added salt tomato paste

1 tablespoon paprika

1 tablespoon cornflour

1 x 375ml can evaporated light milk

pepper to taste

DIRECTIONS

Coat a large non-stick frypan with cooking spray, add garlic and chicken strips, toss together until browned. Add onion to pan and cook 2 minutes, place mushrooms into pan and cook a further 2 minutes. Add gherkins, stock powder, tomato paste, paprika and stir well. Blend cornflour into milk, add to pan stirring continuously until sauce boils, pepper to taste.

VARIATIONS: REPLACE CHICKEN WITH LEAN RUMP STEAK OR WITH VEAL LEG STEAK.

Dietitian's Tip

Removing the skin from the chicken reduced the amount of saturated fat in the recipe making it suitable for people with diabetes.

Nutritional Information

PER SERVE		CHICKEN	RUMP	VEAL
FAT	TOTAL	5.2g	5.7g	2.2g
	SATURATED	1.9g	2.7g	1.2g
FIBRE		2.3g	2.3g	2.3g
PROTEIN		44.5g	45.7g	42.2g
CARBS		16.9g	16.9g	16.9g
SUGAR		14.4g	14.4g	14.4g
SODIUM		274mg	266mg	313mg
KILOJOULES		1238 (cals 295)	1275 (cals 304)	1089 (cals 259)
GI RATING		Low	Low	Low

Chicken Parmigiana

SERVES: 4

4 x 125g skinless chicken breasts

cooking spray

75g 97% fat-free ham slices (Hans®)

4 tablespoons no added salt tomato paste

1 cup 25% reduced-fat grated tasty cheese

DIRECTIONS

Preheat oven 180°C fan forced.

Flatten chicken breasts using a meat mallet. Place on a baking tray that has been coated with cooking spray. Place ham slices evenly on top of each flattened piece of chicken, spread ¼ of tomato paste over each breast, sprinkle cheese on top. Bake 25-30 minutes or until chicken is cooked through. Use egg lifter to place chicken onto plate.

VARIATIONS: REPLACE CHICKEN WITH LEAN VEAL OR LEAN RUMP STEAKS.

Dietitian's Tip

At last a chicken parmigiana that tastes like you find at the pub but without it being high in fat. This is a great choice for people with diabetes who are aiming for weight loss.

Nutritional Information

PER SERVE		CHICKEN	VEAL	RUMP
FAT	TOTAL	9.9g	7.4g	10.3g
	SATURATED	5.1g	4.5g	5.7g
FIBRE		0.2g	0.2g	0.2g
PROTEIN		39.3g	37.5g	40.3g
CARBS		0.8g	0.8g	0.8g
SUGAR		0.7g	0.7g	0.7g
SODIUM		517mg	549mg	511mg
KILOJOULES		984 (cals 234)	860 (cals 205)	1015 (cals 242)
GI RATING			Too low in carbs to score a rating	

Chicken & Mango Bon Bon

SERVES: 4

4 x 125g skinless chicken breasts

½ cup 25% reduced-fat grated tasty cheese

4 shallots

12 sheets filo pastry

cooking spray

1 x 425g can mango slices in natural juice drained or 1 large fresh mango

DIRECTIONS

Preheat oven 180°C fan forced.

Flatten chicken breasts until thin. In centre of each breast of chicken place ¼ of grated cheese, one shallot cut in ½ and 3-4 mango slices. Fold edges of chicken over the filling, leave to one side. Take one sheet filo pastry, spray with cooking spray, place another sheet on top and spray again, place third sheet on top and spray. Place one chicken breast at the start of the pastry in centre, gently rolling down the longest side (like a Swiss roll). Repeat to make 3 more bon bons. Place each bon bon on large baking tray that has been coated with cooking spray. Gently gather or pinch left and right edges together to make shape of a bon bon, spray tops with cooking spray. Bake 30-35 minutes or until golden brown. Serve immediately as filo will soften very quickly. Use a large spatula or egg lifter to serve on plate.

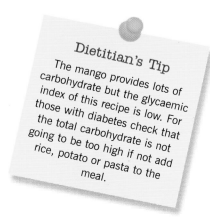

Dietitian's Tip

The mango provides lots of carbohydrate but the glycaemic index of this recipe is low. For those with diabetes check that the total carbohydrate is not going to be too high if not add rice, potato or pasta to the meal.

Nutritional Information

PER BON BON		
FAT	TOTAL	8.3g
	SATURATED	3.8g
FIBRE		1.2g
PROTEIN		38.3g
CARBS		29.4g
SUGAR		7.1g
SODIUM		507mg
KILOJOULES		1460 (cals 348)
GI RATING		Medium

Crunchy Nut Chicken

SERVES: 4

2 cups corn flakes
⅓ cup macadamia nuts finely chopped
½ teaspoon chicken stock powder
1 egg white
¼ cup skim milk
4 x 125g flattened skinless chicken breasts
cooking spray

DIRECTIONS

Preheat oven 180°C fan forced.

Place corn flakes in a plastic bag then using a rolling pin crush finely. Add nuts and stock powder into bag and shake, tip onto a flat plate. Using a fork beat egg white and milk. Dip flattened breasts in egg mixture, then coat each side of chicken with crumbs. Place on a flat baking tray that has been coated with cooking spray, spray over top of chicken and bake 25-30 minutes or until cooked and coating is golden brown.

VARIATION: FOR AN EVEN LOWER FAT COUNT OMIT MACADAMIA NUTS AND ADD ½ CUP MORE CORN FLAKES TO CRUMBS.

Dietitian's Tip
Macadamia nuts add a great taste to this recipe and provide lots of mono and polyunsaturated saturated fat that is need for a healthy heart.

Chicken & Spinach Risotto

SERVES: 6

2 teaspoons (10g) Flora Light® margarine
1 small onion finely diced
1 teaspoon crushed garlic (in jar)
2 cups raw arborio rice
3 cups salt-reduced chicken stock liquid (Campbells®)
2 teaspoons chicken stock powder
3 cups water
250g skinless chicken breast cut into small dice
⅓ cup white wine
3 tablespoons grated parmesan cheese
1 x 250g packet frozen spinach thawed & drained
pepper to taste

DIRECTIONS

You must cook this recipe in a large non-stick saucepan. Melt margarine in pan, cook onion and garlic 2 minutes. Add rice and cook for 3 minutes stirring frequently. Add 2 cups of stock liquid and all stock powder, bring to boil, reduce to a simmer, stir frequently until liquid has been absorbed by rice. Add in raw diced chicken, 1 cup stock liquid, 1 cup water and wine stirring frequently whilst simmering. Once absorbed pour in final 2 cups of water, stirring frequently until absorbed (rice should be cooked by this stage). Stir in parmesan cheese, defrosted spinach, pepper to taste, stir well. Serve.

*Note: Risotto when cooked should have a moist consistency.

VARIATION: REPLACE SPINACH WITH 2½ CUPS MUSHROOMS SLICED.

Dietitian's Tip
This meal is suitable for the active person with diabetes who needs lots of carbohydrate at each meal.

Nutritional Information

PER SERVE		MACADAMIA	W/OUT MACADAMIA
FAT	TOTAL	9.7g	3.0g
	SATURATED	1.7g	0.8g
FIBRE		1.0g	0.5g
PROTEIN		31.4g	30.7g
CARBS		13.9g	13.5g
SUGAR		2.6g	2.2g
SODIUM		269mg	269mg
KILOJOULES		1126 (cals 268)	862 (cals 205)
GI RATING		High	High

Nutritional Information

PER SERVE		
FAT	TOTAL	4.6g
	SATURATED	1.6g
FIBRE		3.9g
PROTEIN		28.1g
CARBS		56.7g
SUGAR		2.7g
SODIUM		470mg
KILOJOULES		1640 (cals 390)
GI RATING		High

Chicken with Pepper Sauce

SERVES: 6

1 tablespoon dried medley peppercorn mix

cooking spray

½ cup onion finely chopped

2 teaspoons salt-reduced chicken-style stock powder (Massel®)

2 tablespoons brandy

¼ cup red wine

3 tablespoons cornflour

½ cup water

1 x 375ml can evaporated light milk

pepper to taste

6 x 150g skinless chicken breasts

Dietitian's Tip
This creamy sauce is surprisingly low in fat due to Annette's cleaver use of evaporated skim milk. People with diabetes who are interested in weight loss will find this recipe delicious.

DIRECTIONS

Crush peppercorns using a rolling pin. Coat a non-stick saucepan with cooking spray, cook onion and crushed peppercorns 2 minutes, stirring continuously. Add chicken stock powder, brandy, red wine and bring to boil. Combine cornflour with water, add to pot and bring to boil. Pour in milk, stir ingredients together well, pepper to taste. Once boiled reduce to a low simmer. Cook chicken breasts by grilling, dry bake or pan fry in a non-stick frypan that has been coated with cooking spray. Spoon pepper sauce over chicken and serve.

VARIATIONS: REPLACE CHICKEN WITH LEAN RUMP OR LEAN BUTTERFLY PORK STEAK.

Nutritional Information

PER SERVE		CHICKEN	RUMP	PORK
FAT	TOTAL	4.5g	5.0g	2.6g
	SATURATED	1.6g	2.4g	1.2g
FIBRE		0.4g	0.4g	0.4g
PROTEIN		39.4g	40.6g	42.1g
CARBS		11.3g	11.3g	11.3g
SUGAR		7.9g	7.9g	7.9g
SODIUM		147mg	139mg	142mg
KILOJOULES		1109 (cals 264)	1147 (cals 273)	1084 (cals 258)
GI RATING		Low	Low	Low

Crumbed Lamb Cutlets

SERVES: 4

- 12 medium size (480g) lean lamb French cutlets
- 1 egg white
- ½ cup skim milk
- 1 cup dried breadcrumbs

Dietitian's Tip
Usually lamb cutlets are deep fried but this recipe uses grilling without added fat making the lean lamb suitable to included in a healthy eating plan for people with diabetes.

DIRECTIONS

Trim cutlets, cutting as much visible fat off as possible. Beat egg white and milk together. Coat each cutlet with egg mix then coat in breadcrumbs. Repeat until all cutlets are crumbed. Place under grill, cook until browned, checking regularly so as not to burn cutlets. Once both sides are browned serve 3 cutlets per person.

NOTE:
To make a low-fat gravy use GRAVOX ® Lite Supreme gravy mix as directed on packet.

Nutritional Information

PER SERVE				
FAT	TOTAL	5.8g	CARBS	11.0g
	SATURATED	2.5g	SUGAR	1.8g
FIBRE		0.6g	SODIUM	177mg
PROTEIN		20.4g	KILOJOULES	747 (cals 178)
			GI RATING	Medium

Green Beef Curry

SERVES: 4

- cooking spray
- 600g lean rump steak (cut into strips)
- 1 teaspoon green curry paste
- ½ teaspoon imitation coconut essence
- 1 can 375ml evaporated light milk
- 1 teaspoon sugar
- 1 teaspoon salt-reduced vegetable stock powder (Massel®)
- 1 tablespoon fresh basil chopped
- 2 teaspoons soy sauce 43% less salt
- 2 teaspoons fish sauce
- 1 teaspoon crushed ginger (in jar)
- 1 teaspoon crushed garlic (in jar)
- 1 cup canned bamboo shoots drained
- 1 cup choko diced
- 1 cup beans sliced
- 1 cup capsicum strips
- 1 cup onion sliced
- 1 tablespoon cornflour
- ¼ cup water

Dietitian's Tip
Coconut essence and skim evaporated milk replace the higher saturated fat coconut milk making the curry a good choice for peoples aiming to lose weight. People with diabetes are advised to use less of the soy sauce to decrease the sodium content.

DIRECTIONS

Coat a wok or frypan with cooking spray, fry rump 3 mins. Add in curry paste and cook 1 more minute. Add all other ingredients except cornflour and water, bring to boil, simmer until all the vegetables are just cooked (about 5 minutes). Combine cornflour and water and add to pan, bring to boil. Serve with rice, noodles or new potatoes.
VARIATIONS: REPLACE RUMP WITH 600g SKINLESS CHICKEN BREAST
OR REPLACE RUMP WITH 600g GREEN PRAWNS
OR REPLACE RUMP WITH 400g TOFU.

Nutritional Information

PER SERVE		RUMP	CHICKEN	TOFU
FAT	TOTAL	6.1g	5.6g	8.2g
	SATURATED	2.7g	2.0g	1.1g
FIBRE		3.1g	3.1g	3.1g
PROTEIN		45.2g	44.0g	20.1g
CARBS		20.0g	20.0g	24.0g
SUGAR		15.6g	15.6g	16.6g
SODIUM		584mg	592mg	515mg
KILOJOULES		1333 (cals 317)	1295 (cals 308)	947 (cals 225)
GI RATING		Low	Low	Low

Veal Napolitana

SERVES: 4

600g veal steak cut into strips

1 teaspoon crushed garlic

cooking spray

2 tablespoons brandy

1 cup onion sliced

2 cups mushrooms sliced

1 cup capsicum cut into strips

1 x 420g can salt-reduced tomato soup (undiluted)

1 x 400g can no added salt tomato puree

2 tablespoons no added salt tomato paste

1 teaspoon beef stock powder

1 teaspoon oregano

pepper to taste

Dietitian's Tip
Tomatoes are great source of vitamin A required for vision and keeping the skin and membranes resistant to infection and promote growth.

DIRECTIONS

Sauté veal and garlic in a large non-stick frypan that has been coated with cooking spray, until browned. Add brandy and cook 1 minute. Add onion, mushrooms, capsicum and cook 2 minutes. Stir in soup, puree, tomato paste, stock powder, oregano and bring to boil, simmer 10 minutes. Pepper to taste.

VARIATIONS: REPLACE VEAL WITH SKINLESS CHICKEN BREAST CUT INTO STRIPS OR RUMP CUT INTO STRIPS.

Nutritional Information

PER SERVE		VEAL	CHICKEN	RUMP
FAT	TOTAL	1.0g	4.0g	4.4g
	SATURATED	0.2g	1.0g	1.7g
FIBRE		3.5g	3.5g	3.5g
PROTEIN		36.1g	38.3g	39.5g
CARBS		16.3g	16.3g	16.3g
SUGAR		11.7g	11.7g	11.7g
SODIUM		463mg	424mg	416mg
KILOJOULES		1000 (cals 238)	1148 (cals 273)	1186 (cals 282)
GI RATING		Low	Low	Low

Sweet & Sour Pork

SERVES: 6

600g new fashioned pork diced

cooking spray

1 onion sliced

1 cup each sliced carrot, green capsicum, celery

½ teaspoon chopped ginger

1 tablespoon soy sauce

1 tablespoon sugar

¼ teaspoon Chinese five-spice

2 teaspoons salt-reduced chicken-style stock powder (Massel®)

1 tablespoon tomato sauce

2 tablespoons tomato paste

½ cup pineapple pieces (no sugar added)

2 tablespoons cornflour

1½ cups pineapple juice (no sugar added)

Dietitian's Tip
The Dietary Guidelines for Australians advise us to reduce added sugar in our eating plan. This sweet tasting recipe has much less sugar than the traditional recipe making it a good choice for people with diabetes.

DIRECTIONS

Brown pork in a non-stick frypan that has been coated with cooking spray. Add onion, carrot, capsicum and celery, cook 5 minutes. Add ginger, soy sauce, sugar, five spice, stock powder, tomato sauce, tomato paste and pineapple pieces. Blend cornflour with pineapple juice, add to pan. Cook a further 5-7 minutes or until vegetables are just cooked. Serve with rice or pasta.

VARIATIONS: REPLACE PORK WITH SKINLESS CHICKEN BREASTS OR REPLACE PORK WITH BONELESS FISH FILLETS CUT INTO LARGE CHUNKS. COOK FISH IN THE LAST 5 MINUTES OF METHOD.

Nutritional Information

PER SERVE		PORK	CHICKEN	FISH
FAT	TOTAL	1.2g	2.5g	0.9g
	SATURATED	0.3g	0.6g	0.2g
FIBRE		1.8g	1.8g	1.8g
PROTEIN		25.8g	24.0g	21.2g
CARBS		18.2g	18.2g	18.2g
SUGAR		15.4g	15.4g	15.4g
SODIUM		295mg	298mg	313mg
KILOJOULES		782 (cals 186)	799 (cals 190)	692 (cals 165)
GI RATING		Medium	Medium	Medium

Macaroni Beef

SERVES: 6

MEAT SAUCE

600g very lean beef mince

cooking spray

¾ cup carrot grated

¾ cup zucchini grated

1 small onion finely diced

½ cup frozen peas

1 x 420g can salt-reduced tomato soup (undiluted)

2 teaspoons salt-reduced chicken-style stock powder (Massel®)

2 tablespoons no added salt tomato paste

3 cups cooked macaroni noodles

TOPPING

1 tablespoon (15g) Flora Light® margarine

3 tablespoons plain flour

1½ cups skim milk

¾ cup 25% reduced-fat grated tasty cheese

Dietitian's Tip
The carbohydrate in the macaroni noodles is absorbed slowly into the body. This will give insulin ample time to take the sugar out of the blood and into the cells.

DIRECTIONS

Preheat oven 180ºC fan forced.

To make meat sauce:

Cook mince in a large non-stick saucepan that has been coated with cooking spray. Drain liquid then return mince to pot. Add in carrots, zucchini, onion, peas and soup, cook 2 minutes stirring continuously. Add stock powder and tomato paste, cook a further 5 minutes stirring frequently. Fold in cooked macaroni noodles and mix together well. Pour mixture into a lasagne dish.

To make topping:

Melt margarine in saucepan, add flour, cook 1 minute. Slowly add milk using a whisk to avoid lumps, stir continuously until boiling. Pour sauce over the meat, sprinkle with grated cheese. Bake 25-30 minutes or until top is golden brown.

VARIATION: OMIT TOPPING.

Nutritional Information

PER SERVE		WITH TOPPING	WITHOUT
FAT	TOTAL	7.5g	3.2g
	SATURATED	3.3g	1.1g
FIBRE		4.7g	4.5g
PROTEIN		34.9g	28.5g
CARBS		35.1g	28.8g
SUGAR		11.7g	8.4g
SODIUM		422mg	294mg
KILOJOULES		1458 (cals 347)	1085 (cals 258)
GI RATING		Low	Low

Rib Fillet Forestiere

SERVES: 4

cooking spray

2 cups mushrooms quartered

¾ cup 97% fat-free ham (Hans®) in large dice

1 x 150g jar white cocktail onions (drained)

2 tablespoons brandy

¼ cup red wine

1 tablespoon salt-reduced vegetable stock powder (Massel®)

1½ cups water

3 tablespoons cornflour

pepper to taste

4 x 150g lean rib fillet steaks

Dietitian's Tip
People with diabetes and high blood pressure may like to add less ham and stock powder to reduce the sodium content of the recipe.

DIRECTIONS

Coat a non-stick saucepan with cooking spray, add mushrooms, ham and onions, cook 2 minutes stirring continuously. Add brandy and red wine, bring to boil, add stock powder with 1 cup water (leaving ½ cup of water to be mixed with cornflour later), simmer 5 minutes stirring occasionally. Blend cornflour into remaining ½ cup water, add to pot and bring to boil, stir ingredients well, pepper to taste. Once boiled reduce to a low simmer.

To cook rib fillets either grill or pan fry to preferred liking e.g. rare, medium or well done. Spoon forestiere sauce equally over fillets and serve.

VARIATIONS: REPLACE RIB FILLET WITH LEAN RUMP STEAK, BUTTERFLY PORK STEAK, SKINLESS CHICKEN BREAST.

Nutritional Information

PER SERVE	RIB	RUMP	CHICKEN	PORK
FAT TOTAL	6.4g	4.6g	4.1g	2.2g
SATURATED	2.6g	1.9g	1.1g	0.7g
FIBRE	1.3g	1.3g	1.3g	1.3g
PROTEIN	36.9g	39.6g	38.4g	41.1g
CARBS	9.7g	9.7g	9.7g	9.7g
SUGAR	4.0g	4.0g	4.0g	4.0g
SODIUM	573mg	568mg	576mg	571mg
KILOJOULES	1086 (cals 259)	1065 (cals 254)	1028 (cals 245)	1002 (cals 239)
GI RATING	Low	Low	Low	Low

Steak Diane

SERVES: 6

cooking spray

2 teaspoons crushed garlic (in jar)

1 cup shallots chopped

2 tablespoons brandy

½ cup red wine

2 teaspoons salt-reduced chicken-style stock powder (Massel®)

2 tablespoons Worcestershire sauce

3 tablespoons cornflour

½ cup water

1 x 375ml can evaporated light milk

pepper to taste

6 x 150g flattened lean rump steaks

DIRECTIONS

Coat a non-stick saucepan with cooking spray, cook garlic and shallots 2 minutes stirring continuously. Add brandy, red wine, stock powder and Worcestershire sauce, bring to boil and simmer 3 minutes stirring occasionally. Mix cornflour with water, add to pot and bring to boil, stir ingredients well. Add milk, pepper to taste, bring back to boil, reduce to a low simmer.

Dietitian's Tip
Cream is not added to this recipe. The use of evaporated light milk and cornflour makes the creamy taste and lowers the fat content making the sauce suitable for people with diabetes.

To cook rump, grill or pan fry to preferred liking e.g. rare, medium or well done. Spoon diane sauce equally over each rump and serve.

VARIATIONS: REPLACE RUMP WITH LEAN RIB FILLET OR SKINLESS CHICKEN BREAST.

Nutritional Information

PER SERVE	RUMP	RIB	CHICKEN
FAT TOTAL	5.0g	6.8g	4.5g
SATURATED	2.4g	3.1g	1.6g
FIBRE	0.4g	0.4g	0.4g
PROTEIN	40.8g	38.1g	39.6g
CARBS	12.6g	12.6g	12.6g
SUGAR	9.1g	9.1g	9.1g
SODIUM	234mg	238mg	241mg
KILOJOULES	1206 (cals 287)	1227 (cals 292)	1168 (cals 278)
GI RATING	Low	Low	Low

Steak with Mushroom Sauce

SERVES: 4

cooking spray

2½ cups Swiss brown mushrooms sliced

½ cup onion sliced

2 tablespoons brandy

¼ cup red wine

3 teaspoons salt-reduced chicken-style stock powder (Massel®)

1½ cups water

3 tablespoons cornflour

pepper to taste

4 x 150g lean rump steaks

Dietitian's Tip
Loaded with important nutrients including iron and Vitamin B12 makes this an outstanding meal for the whole family including people with diabetes.

DIRECTIONS

Coat a non-stick saucepan with cooking spray, sauté mushrooms and onion 2 minutes stirring continuously. Add brandy and red wine, bring to boil. Add stock powder and 1 cup water (leaving ½ cup of water to be mixed with cornflour later), simmer 5 minutes stirring occasionally. Mix cornflour with ½ cup water, add to pot, bring to boil stirring well, pepper to taste. Once boiled reduce to a low simmer.

Cut all visible fat off rump steak and grill to preferred liking e.g. rare, medium or well done.

Spoon mushroom sauce equally over rump steaks and serve.

VARIATIONS: REPLACE RUMP WITH 4 x 150g OF EITHER LEAN BUTTERFLY PORK STEAKS, VEAL STEAKS OR SKINLESS CHICKEN BREASTS.

Nutritional Information

PER SERVE	RUMP	CHICKEN	PORK	VEAL
FAT TOTAL	4.3g	3.8g	1.9g	0.8g
SATURATED	1.7g	1.0g	0.5g	0.2g
FIBRE	1.3g	1.3g	1.3g	1.3g
PROTEIN	37.2g	36.0g	38.7g	33.8g
CARBS	6.9g	6.9g	6.9g	6.9g
SUGAR	0.8g	0.8g	0.8g	0.8g
SODIUM	451mg	458mg	454mg	497mg
KILOJOULES	1026 (cals 244)	988 (cals 235)	963 (cals 229)	840 (cals 200)
GI RATING			Too low in carbs to score a rating	

Steak Pie

SERVES: 4

cooking spray

750g lean stewing beef diced

1 cup onion cut into large dice

1½ cups water

2 tablespoons Worcestershire sauce

3 teaspoons salt-reduced chicken-style stock powder (Massel®)

3 tablespoons plain flour

7 sheets filo pastry

Dietitian's Tip
Filo pastry is low in fat and makes a great pie. This and the lean meat pie filling make the recipe suitable for people with diabetes.

DIRECTIONS

Brown beef in non-stick saucepan tha with cooking spray. Drain liquid, add onion stirring together for 3 minutes. Add 1¼ cups of water (leaving remaining ¼ cup to blend with flour later), add Worcestershire sauce and stock powder, bring to the boil, reduce to a simmer for 30 minutes with lid on, stirring occasionally. Blend flour with remaining water and stir into pot, boil 2-3 minutes or until sauce thickens. Leave filling to cool.

Preheat oven 200°C fan forced.

Spray a pie dish (20cm) with cooking spray. Cut filo sheets in half (use 8 for base, 6 for top). Layer pie dish with 8 cut sheets, in a rotating fashion, spraying with cooking spray between each sheet. Spoon meat mixture on top of pastry. Place remaining filo sheets by layering over top of filling in a rotating fashion, spraying with cooking spray between sheets. Crinkle edges together, spray with cooking spray. Bake 30-35 minutes or until golden brown. Serve immediately as pastry will soften when left. To crisp again either place back in oven or under grill.

VARIATION: FOR STEAK AND KIDNEY PIE REPLACE STEWING BEEF WITH 500g STEAK DICED AND 250g KIDNEY DICED.

Nutritional Information

PER SERVE	STEAK	STEAK/KIDNEY
FAT TOTAL	7.6g	6.8g
SATURATED	3.1g	2.7g
FIBRE	1.0g	1.0g
PROTEIN	44.1g	41.3g
CARBS	20.4g	20.4g
SUGAR	2.8g	2.8g
SODIUM	369mg	451mg
KILOJOULES	1371 (cals 326)	1296 (cals 308)
GI RATING	Medium	Medium

Shepherd's Pie

SERVES: 6 LARGE OR 8 AVERAGE

1 onion diced

1 cup each of carrot diced, zucchini and celery sliced

1 cup each of small broccoli and cauliflower florets

½ cup each of frozen peas, corn kernels and green bean slices

600g very lean mince

cooking spray

2 teaspoons salt-reduced chicken-style stock powder (Massel®)

½ cup Gravox® Lite Supreme

2 tablespoons tomato sauce

2 tablespoons Worcestershire sauce

2 tablespoons oyster sauce

3 cups water

POTATO TOP

1 kilo potatoes (about 8 medium)

¼ cup skim milk

½ cup 25% reduced-fat grated tasty cheese

Dietitian's Tip

The potato provides ample carbohydrate for people with diabetes. To make this a complete meal simply add tomato sauce and green vegetables.

DIRECTIONS

Microwave all the vegetables in a little water on high for 10 minutes.

Cook mince in large saucepan or boiler that has been coated with cooking spray. Once cooked drain, return mince to saucepan, add stock powder, Gravox® powder, tomato sauce, Worcestershire and oyster sauce plus water, stir together well. Once boiled add in pre-cooked drained vegetables, put lid on and simmer for 5 minutes, stirring occasionally (be careful that mixture does not stick to base of pot). Leave in saucepan.

To make potato top: Peel and dice potatoes. Microwave in a little water until cooked (about 12-15 minutes). Once cooked drain, mash with skim milk.

Re-heat mince mixture then pour into a large lasagne dish. Using a spoon and fork put small dobs of mashed potato over top of meat; run a fork over top to blend potato evenly. Sprinkle with grated cheese, place under grill until browned on top.

Nutritional Information

PER SERVE		LARGE	AVERAGE
FAT	TOTAL	9.9g	7.4g
	SATURATED	4.3g	3.2g
FIBRE		7.0g	5.3g
PROTEIN		31.2g	23.4g
CARBS		34.0g	25.5g
SUGAR		8.1g	6.1g
SODIUM		585mg	439mg
KILOJOULES		1476 (cals 351)	1107 (cals 264)
GI RATING		High	High

Hamburgers

SERVES: 6

500g very lean beef mince

½ small onion finely diced

1 egg white

2 tablespoons tomato sauce

2 tablespoons BBQ sauce

pepper to taste

cooking spray

6 multigrain breadrolls (50g each)

salad: e.g. cucumber, tomato, grated carrot, beetroot, shredded lettuce

Dietitian's Tip

This is a complete meal that includes a variety of foods, is low in fat, high in protein and the carbohydrate has a low glycaemic index. This is an ideal great meal for people with diabetes.

DIRECTIONS

In a large mixing bowl place mince, onion, egg white, tomato sauce, BBQ sauce, pepper to taste. Mix together using your hands until well combined. Divide into 6 round shaped patties, flatten slightly. Generously coat a large frypan with cooking spray. Fry burgers until cooked on both sides. Cut buns in half, grill until toasted brown. Place salad of your choice on base of bun then top with meat patties, place bun lid on top.

Nutritional Information

PER HAMBURGER		
FAT	TOTAL	8.0g
	SATURATED	2.7g
FIBRE		5.3g
PROTEIN		23.7g
CARBS		31.2g
SUGAR		7.8g
SODIUM		479mg
KILOJOULES		1226 (cals 292)
GI RATING		Low

Christmas

Christmas Pudding

SERVES: 16

7 slices multigrain bread (crumble including crusts)

1 cup skim milk

3 cups (500g) mixed fruit

2 teaspoons mixed spice

½ cup rum or brandy

3 egg whites

¾ teaspoon bicarb soda

½ cup apple sauce (in jar)

1 cup mashed banana

1 tablespoon Parisian essence (optional)

1¼ cups plain flour

cooking spray

DIRECTIONS

Put breadcrumbs in a large mixing bowl, heat milk until hot, then pour over breadcrumbs, stir together until really mushy and bread has absorbed all the milk. Add in mixed fruit, spices and rum/brandy, mix together well. Beat egg whites into mixture well. Mix bicarb soda with apple sauce (it will froth) then add to bowl. Stir in mashed banana and parisian essence (this will make a darker pudding). Fold in flour and mix until all ingredients are well combined.

Pour into a 19cm x 9 cm pudding steamer that has been sprayed with cooking spray, spray lid as well. Secure lid.

Put a saucer turned upside down into boiler, put pudding dish on top of saucer and fill with boiling water which reaches ¾ of the way up the steamer. Steam in a covered boiler simmering for 4 hours. Check water level occasionally, top up if needed.

To reheat place in boiler for 1 hour before serving.

Dietitian's Tip
A special occasion pudding that is low in fat but high in carbohydrate and kilojoules. The whole family will enjoy this at Christmas lunch.

Yule Time Muffins

MAKES: 12

cooking spray

2 egg whites

½ teaspoon vanilla essence

¼ cup sugar

½ teaspoon bicarb soda

½ cup apple sauce (in jar)

½ cup skim milk

⅔ cup fruit mince

2 cups self-raising flour

Dietitian's Tip
These muffins are ideal for that very special occasion. They are packed with carbohydrate and kilojoules but low in fat making one ample - avoid seconds.

DIRECTIONS

Preheat oven 200°C fan forced.

Coat a 12 cup muffin tray with cooking spray. Beat egg whites, essence and sugar for 1 minute in a medium size mixing bowl. Stir bicarb soda into apple sauce (it will froth) then add to bowl with milk and fruit mince, mixing well. Gently fold sifted flour into mixture in one go, treat this mixture as if a sponge, DO NOT BEAT as this will make the muffins tough. Spoon mixture into prepared muffin pan dividing equally into 12 cups. Bake for 15-20 minutes or until firm to touch. Allow muffins to sit in tin for 5 minutes before turning onto a wire rack to cool.

Nutritional Information

PER SERVE		
FAT	TOTAL	0.8g
	SATURATED	0.2g
FIBRE		3.1g
PROTEIN		4.4g
CARBS		39.4g
SUGAR		25.6g
SODIUM		153mg
KILOJOULES		823 (cals 196)
GI RATING		Low

Nutritional Information

PER MUFFIN		
FAT	TOTAL	0.9g
	SATURATED	0.2g
FIBRE		1.6g
PROTEIN		4.1g
CARBS		35.8g
SUGAR		14.8g
SODIUM		273mg
KILOJOULES		702 (cals 167)
GI RATING		Medium

Christmas Cake

SERVES: 16

1 cup sultanas
½ cup raisins
½ cup currants
½ cup (100g) glace cherries (cut in ½)
⅓ cup mixed peel
⅓ cup raw sugar
2 teaspoons mixed spice
1 cup water
¾ teaspoon bicarb soda
1 cup mashed pumpkin (250g raw)
3 egg whites
½ cup brandy or rum
2 cups self-raising flour
cooking spray
¼ cup (30g) whole blanched almonds (optional)

DIRECTIONS

Place dried fruit, sugar, spice and water in a saucepan, boil 3 minutes. Stir in bicarb soda, leave to cool. Boil or microwave pumpkin, drain and mash, leave to cool.

Preheat oven 180°C fan forced.

Mix pumpkin and fruit mix together, beat in egg whites. Add brandy, then add flour in one go to fruit mix and gently fold until ingredients are combined. Pour mixture into a cake tin that has been coated with cooking spray. Decorate top of cake with almonds (optional). Bake 55-60 minutes.

In hot/humid weather it is best to keep cake refrigerated.

VARIATIONS: TO MAKE AN EASIER CHRISTMAS CAKE REPLACE SULTANAS, RAISINS, CURRANTS, MIXED PEEL AND GLACE CHERRIES WITH 3 CUPS 500g DRIED MIXED FRUIT
OR FOR AN EVEN LOWER FAT COUNT OMIT ALMONDS.

Dietitian's Tip
Lots of fruit, fibre, carbohydrate and kilojoules. Christmas comes but once a year and for people aiming to lose weight or with diabetes having this cake once a year is enough.

Nutritional Information

PER SERVE		ALMONDS	W/OUT ALMONDS
FAT	TOTAL	1.4g	0.4g
	SATURATED	0.2g	0.1g
FIBRE		2.1g	1.9g
PROTEIN		3.6g	3.2g
CARBS		38.2g	25.1g
SUGAR		25.2g	25.1g
SODIUM		199mg	199mg
KILOJOULES		812 (cals 193)	765 (cals 182)
GI RATING		Medium	Medium

Fruit Mince Pies

MAKES: 12

1½ cups self-raising flour
¼ cup sugar
2 tablespoons (30g) Flora Light® margarine
⅓ cup skim milk
1 egg white
flour to roll out pastry
cooking spray
12 tablespoons fruit mince (in jar)
1-2 teaspoons sugar

DIRECTIONS

Preheat oven 180°C fan forced.

In a large mixing bowl combine flour and ¼ cup sugar together. Melt margarine and add to milk; using a fork beat one egg white into milk mixture. Pour into flour and fold together. Place pastry on a lightly floured surface, knead lightly. Divide in 2; roll out first ½ until big enough to cut out 12 bases (8cm cutter). Gently place into 12 muffin tins that have been coated with cooking spray. Spoon 1 tablespoon of fruit mince mixture into centre of each pastry case. Roll out remaining pastry as for base, then place pastry circles over top of fruit mix. Lightly brush tops with a little extra egg white then sprinkle lightly with 1-2 teaspoons sugar. Bake 20-25 minutes or until pies are golden brown.

Dietitian's Tip
These pies are ideal for that very special occasion. They are packed with carbohydrate and kilojoules but low in fat making one ample - avoid seconds.

Nutritional Information

PER PIE		
FAT	TOTAL	2.1g
	SATURATED	0.5g
FIBRE		1.4g
PROTEIN		2.9g
CARBS		28.1g
SUGAR		13.5g
SODIUM		170mg
KILOJOULES		591 (cals 141)
GI RATING		Medium

Tropical Christmas Cake

SERVES: 16

3 cups (500g) mixed dried fruit

½ cup brown sugar

1 teaspoon mixed spice

½ cup brandy or rum

1 x 440g crushed pineapple (in natural juice)

¾ teaspoon bicarb soda

3 egg whites

1 tablespoon Parisian essence (gravy browner) (optional)

2 cups self-raising flour

cooking spray

¼ cup (30g) whole blanched almonds (optional)

Dietitian's Tip

People with diabetes may require a smaller serving size, as the cake is high in carbohydrate and kilojoules.

DIRECTIONS

Place mixed fruit, sugar, spice, brandy and whole can of pineapple into a saucepan, boil for 3 minutes. Stir in bicarb soda, leave to cool.

Preheat oven 180°C fan forced.

Once fruit mixture has cooled stir in egg whites well. If you prefer a darker cake add in Parisian essence to fruit mix then fold in flour. Pour mixture into a 19cm (8") round tin that has been coated with cooking spray. Top with almonds and bake approximately 1 hour.

Christmas Strudel

SERVES: 8

1 x 800g can pie apple (no added sugar)

½ teaspoon mixed spice

¾ cup fruit mince (in jar)

8 sheets filo pastry

cooking spray

1 teaspoon sugar

Dietitian's Tip

High in kilojoules and carbs. A small serve is recommended for people with diabetes.

DIRECTIONS

Preheat oven 200°C fan forced.

Combine apple, mixed spice and fruit mince in a medium size mixing bowl. Place one sheet of filo pastry on top of the other spraying each sheet with cooking spray until 8 sheets have been used. Place apple filling along centre of pastry. Spray edges with cooking spray then fold right and left edges inwards, spray again, roll up pastry and filling carefully. Place strudel with the fold side underneath on a baking tray that has been coated with cooking spray. Sprinkle sugar over strudel, pierce top to let out steam. Bake 30-40 minutes or until golden brown. Serve with low-fat custard, low-fat cream or low-fat vanilla ice-cream.

Serve immediately as pastry will soften when left. To crisp again either place back in oven or under grill.

Nutritional Information

PER SERVE		ALMONDS	W/OUT ALMONDS
FAT	TOTAL	1.6g	0.5g
	SATURATED	0.2g	0.1g
FIBRE		3.0g	2.8g
PROTEIN		3.5g	3.2g
CARBS		40.3g	40.2g
SUGAR		27.4g	27.3g
SODIUM		210mg	210mg
KILOJOULES		851 (cals 203)	805 (cals 192)
GI RATING		Low	Low

Nutritional Information

PER SERVE		
FAT	TOTAL	1.2g
	SATURATED	0.3g
FIBRE		2.0g
PROTEIN		2.1g
CARBS		31.6g
SUGAR		23.2g
SODIUM		123mg
KILOJOULES		600 (cals 143)
GI RATING		Low

Desserts

Dietitian's Tip: The recipes featured in this section are good alternatives to traditional high-fat desserts, however it is important to look at your overall daily intake and try and keep 'extras' and excess kilojoules to a minimum if you wish to obtain good health. This section is high in kilojoules and should be chosen as a treat, not a daily occurrence. The best dessert you can have is fruit but when a special occasion arises these recipes are ideal.

Strawberry Chiffon

SERVES: 8

- 1 cup CHILLED evaporated light milk
- ½ teaspoon vanilla essence
- 2 x 150g tubs 99% fat-free vanilla fromage frais (Fruche®)
- 1 sachet (10g) gelatine
- ¼ cup boiling water
- ¾ cup strawberry topping

Dietitian's Tip
A great choice for people with diabetes.

In a large mixing bowl combine chilled milk and essence. Using an electric beater whip milk (3-4 minutes) until thick. Add in Fruche® and beat until combined. Dissolve gelatine in a cup with boiling water stirring well. Mix together with topping, pour into milk mixture and beat until all ingredients are well combined. Pour into serving bowls and refrigerate until set.

Fruche® is a registered trademark of National Foods Limited

VARIATIONS: ADD A PUNNET OF CHOPPED FRESH STRAWBERRIES TO MIXTURE
OR OMIT FRUCHE® AND REPLACE WITH ½ BATCH SYMPLY SWEET CREAM (BOOK 3).

Nutritional Information

PER SERVE				
FAT	TOTAL	0.7g	CARBS	20.9g
	SATURATED	0.4g	SUGAR	20.5g
			SODIUM	57mg
FIBRE		0.1g	KILOJOULES	503 (cals 120)
PROTEIN		7.8g	GI RATING	Low

Strawberry Savoiardi

SERVES: 8

BASE

- 10 savoiardi sponge fingers
- ½ cup fresh orange juice (no sugar added)

STRAWBERRY FILLING

- 1 cup evaporated light milk
- ½ teaspoon vanilla essence
- 1 sachet (10g) gelatine
- ¼ cup boiling water
- ½ cup strawberry topping
- 1 punnet (250g) strawberries

TOP LAYER

- 2 sachets diet strawberry jelly (Cottees®)
- 1 cup boiling water
- 1 cup cold water

DIRECTIONS

Dietitian's Tip
This fruit dessert is low in fat and has a low glycaemic index making it a great choice for people with diabetes.

Place sponge fingers evenly over base of a small lasagne dish, spoon orange juice over top of each finger.

To make filling: In a large mixing bowl add milk and essence, using an electric beater whip milk 2 minutes until thick. Dissolve gelatine powder into ¼ cup boiling water, stir until all gelatine has dissolved. Pour into topping and mix well. Blend topping mix with whipped milk, beat until well combined. Pour over top of sponge fingers, refrigerate until set. Hull and slice strawberries, position on top of filling.

To make top layer: Dissolve jelly crystals with boiling water, stirring until crystals are completely dissolved. Add cold water and mix well, refrigerate. Once jelly has just started to set pour over strawberries and refrigerate until set. When set cut into 8 slices.

Nutritional Information

PER SERVE		
FAT	TOTAL	1.2g
	SATURATED	0.5g
FIBRE		0.9g
PROTEIN		5.5g
CARBS		21.5g
SUGAR		18.2g
SODIUM		82mg
KILOJOULES		492 (cals 117)
GI RATING		Low

Sunshine Pie

SERVES: 12

BASE

9 arrowroot biscuits

9 ginger nut biscuits

¼ cup pineapple juice (from drained canned pineapple)

cooking spray

FILLING

1 x 250g tub low-fat cottage cheese

1 cup sweetened condensed skim milk

1 x 200g tub low-fat natural yoghurt

¾ cup well-drained crushed pineapple (in natural juice)

¼ cup passionfruit pulp

1 sachet (10g) gelatine

¼ cup boiling water

DIRECTIONS

To make base: Put one large freezer bag into another bag (double thickness) and place biscuits into middle. Using a rolling pin crush biscuits until fine crumbs form or alternately place biscuits in food processor and crush this way. Place crumbs in a medium size mixing bowl, slowly add reserved juice mixing well. Coat a pie dish (23cm) with cooking spray, press mixture into dish, use your hand or the back of a spoon to press base evenly over bottom of pie dish, making sure there are no cracks. Refrigerate.

To make filling: Blend cottage cheese in a food processor or blender until smooth. Add condensed milk and yoghurt, blend a few minutes more until combined, pour mixture into a large mixing bowl. Fold in well-drained pineapple and passionfruit pulp. Add gelatine to boiling water, stirring until gelatine is completely dissolved then pour into filling and combine well. Pour evenly over prepared biscuit base and refrigerate until set.

VARIATION: REPLACE PINEAPPLE WITH TINNED MANGO SLICES (IN NATURAL JUICE) WELL DRAINED

Nutritional Information

PER SERVE		
FAT	TOTAL	2.2g
	SATURATED	1.1g
FIBRE		1.2g
PROTEIN		8.2g
CARBS		28.0g
SUGAR		22.6g
SODIUM		109mg
KILOJOULES		679 (cals 162)
GI RATING		Medium

Bread & Butter Pudding

SERVES: 10

3 whole eggs

3 egg whites

4 tablespoons sugar

1 teaspoon vanilla essence

1 litre skim milk

2 tablespoons sultanas (optional)

1½ teaspoons (7.5g) Flora Light® margarine

2 teaspoons raspberry jam

3 slices multigrain bread

nutmeg

DIRECTIONS

Preheat oven 180°C fan forced.

Using an electric beater beat all eggs and whites, sugar and vanilla essence 30 seconds. Add milk and beat again for 1 minute. Pour into a casserole dish (23cm), sprinkle sultanas over egg mixture (optional). Spread margarine and jam over each slice of bread then cut each slice into 2, place over top of custard then sprinkle generously with nutmeg. Place in baking tray that has been ½ filled with water. Bake 1 hour or until firm to touch in centre.

Nutritional Information

PER SERVE		
FAT	TOTAL	2.2g
	SATURATED	0.7g
FIBRE		0.5g
PROTEIN		7.4g
CARBS		15.5g
SUGAR		12.2g
SODIUM		125mg
KILOJOULES		457 (cals 109)
GI RATING		Low

Cherry Heaven

SERVES: 6

2 x 150g tubs 99% fat-free vanilla fromage frais (Fruche®)

1 x 200g tub diet vanilla yoghurt

1 x 420g can pitted black cherries drained

1 chilled Cherry Ripe® chocolate bar (55g)

¾ teaspoon imitation coconut essence

DIRECTIONS

In a medium size mixing bowl combine Fruche® and yoghurt together. Cut cherries in ½, then add to bowl. Grate Cherry Ripe bar and place into mixture with essence. Stir ingredients together. Refrigerate until required.

Fruche® is a registered trademark of National Foods Limited

Dietitian's Tip
The Dietary Guidelines for Adult Australians recommend 2 fruit and 2 to 3 dairy a day. This dessert provides a serve of each making it a nutritious dessert for the whole family.

Nutritional Information

PER SERVE		
FAT	TOTAL	2.4g
	SATURATED	1.8g
FIBRE		1.3g
PROTEIN		8.4g
CARBS		22.8g
SUGAR		21.8g
SODIUM		50mg
KILOJOULES		633 (cals 151)
GI RATING		Low

Baked Custard

SERVES: 8

3 whole eggs

3 egg whites

4 tablespoons sugar

1 teaspoon vanilla essence

1 litre skim milk

nutmeg

DIRECTIONS

Preheat oven 180°C fan forced.

Using an electric beater beat all eggs and whites, sugar and vanilla essence together for 30 seconds. Add in milk and beat again for 1 minute. Pour into a casserole dish (23cm), sprinkle top generously with nutmeg. Place dish into a baking tray that has been ½ filled with water. Bake 1 hour or until firm to touch in centre.

Dietitian's Tip
This custard is lower in kilojoules and fat than the traditional recipe and is high in vitamins and minerals making it an excellent choice for people with diabetes.

Nutritional Information

PER SERVE		
FAT	TOTAL	2.0g
	SATURATED	0.7g
FIBRE		0g
PROTEIN		8.3g
CARBS		11.8g
SUGAR		11.8g
SODIUM		101mg
KILOJOULES		402 (cals 96)
GI RATING		Low

Sticky Date Pudding

SERVES: 8

PUDDING
cooking spray
2 egg whites
¼ cup brown sugar (loosely packed)
½ teaspoon bicarb soda
½ cup apple sauce (in jar)
½ cup seeded dates chopped
1½ cups self-raising flour
SAUCE
1 tablespoon (15g) Flora Light® margarine
¼ cup brown sugar (loosely packed)
½ cup evaporated light milk

DIRECTIONS

Preheat oven 200ºC fan forced.

To make pudding: Coat an 8 cup muffin tin (or 12 cup tray will do) with cooking spray. Using an electric beater beat egg whites and brown sugar for 1 minute in a medium size mixing bowl. Stir bicarb soda into apple sauce (it will froth) then add to bowl with chopped dates, combine ingredients. Gently fold flour into mixture in one go, treat as if a sponge, DO NOT BEAT as this will make the puddings tough (mixture can look a little lumpy). Spoon mixture into prepared muffin pan, dividing equally into 8 cups. Bake 20 minutes or until cooked.

To make sauce: Use a small non-stick saucepan, melt margarine, add sugar to pan and stir until sugar has dissolved. Slowly add in milk. Pour sauce over top of each pudding. Serve with low-fat custard, low-fat cream or low-fat ice-cream.

> **Dietitian's Tip**
> Many people with diabetes would find this dessert higher in kilojoules and carbohydrates than is generally recommended for a healthy eating plan. If you plan to eat this your blood glucose level may raise.

Nutritional Information

PER SERVE		
FAT	TOTAL	1.5g
	SATURATED	0.4g
FIBRE		1.9g
PROTEIN		5.0g
CARBS		39.7g
SUGAR		20.8g
SODIUM		292mg
KILOJOULES		805 (cals 192)
GI RATING		Medium

Golden Syrup Pudding

SERVES: 8

2 egg whites
¼ cup sugar
½ teaspoon bicarb soda
½ cup apple sauce (in jar)
1¼ cups self-raising flour
cooking spray
16 teaspoons golden syrup

DIRECTIONS

Preheat oven 180ºC fan forced.

In a medium size mixing bowl beat egg whites and sugar with an electric beater. Stir bicarb soda into apple sauce (it will froth), add to bowl. Gently fold sifted flour into mixture in one go, treat this mixture as if a sponge, DO NOT BEAT as this will make the puddings tough. Coat 8 tea cups (rounded are best) with cooking spray then pour 2 teaspoons of golden syrup into each cup, pour pudding mixture evenly into the 8 cups. Put cups into a baking tray that has been ½ filled with water. Bake 20-25 minutes or until firm to touch in centre. Once cooked remove from water and turn upside down into individual dessert bowls. Serve with low-fat custard, low-fat cream or low-fat ice cream.

VARIATIONS: TO MAKE INDIVIDUAL JAM PUDDINGS REPLACE QUANTITIES OF GOLDEN SYRUP WITH JAM OF YOUR CHOICE OR FOR A LOWER SUGAR COUNT REPLACE JAM WITH COTTEES® DIET JAM.

> **Dietitian's Tip**
> If you have diabetes make the "Diet Jam" option because this decreases both the carbohydrate and kilojoule content of the pudding. This will be better for weight and blood glucose control.

Nutritional Information

PER SERVE		G/SYRUP	JAM	DIET JAM
FAT	TOTAL	0.3g	0.3g	0.3g
	SATURATED	0g	0g	0g
FIBRE		0.8g	1.0g	1.0g
PROTEIN		3.2g	3.2g	3.2g
CARBS		35.5g	33.5g	25.0g
SUGAR		19.7g	17.7g	9.1g
SODIUM		256mg	238mg	245mg
KILOJOULES		651 (cals 155)	622 (cals 148)	487 (cals 116)
GI RATING		Medium	Medium	Medium

Pavlova

SERVES: 8

cooking spray

2 teaspoons cornflour

4 egg whites

¾ cup caster sugar

¼ cup almond flakes (optional)

2 x 150g tubs 99% fat-free vanilla fromage frais (Fruche®)

1 punnet (250g) strawberries sliced

2 passionfruits

DIRECTIONS

Preheat oven 170°C fan forced.

Coat a non-stick baking tray with cooking spray, shake cornflour over base, removing any extra. In a large mixing bowl beat egg whites with an electric beater until stiff peaks form. Gradually add in sugar, beating well each time until sugar dissolves. Spread pavlova mixture in centre of tray to form a round 20cm size. Position almonds around side edges of pavlova. Bake for approximately 45 minutes. Once pavlova has cooled use a large spatula to lift pavlova onto a large plate, spread Fruche® evenly over top, decorate with strawberries and drained passionfruit.

Fruche® is a registered trademark of National Foods Limited

VARIATIONS: FOR AN EVEN LOWER FAT COUNT OMIT ALMOND FLAKES
OR REPLACE FRUCHE® WITH 1 BATCH SYMPLE SWEET CREAM (BOOK 3)
OR REPLACE FRUIT WITH ANY FRESH FRUIT YOU PREFER E.G. BANANA, KIWI, RASPBERRIES, BLUEBERRIES, MANGO.

Dietitian's Tip
This pavlova has much less fat than traditional recipes. This is great but the nutrient level is low and the carbohydrate and sugar intake high so I advise people with diabetes to avoid this pavlova or have it very occasionally.

Nutritional Information

PER SERVE		FRUCHE	SYMPLE SWEET CREAM
FAT	TOTAL	1.6g	2.2g
	SATURATED	0.2g	0.6g
FIBRE		1.6g	1.6g
PROTEIN		7.0g	13.9g
CARBS		26.2g	28.9g
SUGAR		25.6g	28.4g
SODIUM		45mg	111mg
KILOJOULES		623 (cals 148)	785 (cals 187)
GI RATING		Medium	Medium

Lemon Meringue Pie

SERVES: 10

PASTRY

1 cup self-raising flour

1 tablespoon sugar

1 tablespoon (15g) Flora Light® margarine

2 tablespoons skim milk

1 egg white

flour to roll pastry

cooking spray

FILLING

½ cup fresh lemon juice

½ cup sugar

½ cup water

5 level tablespoons custard powder

½ cup evaporated light milk

MERINGUE

3 egg whites

¾ cup caster sugar

DIRECTIONS

Preheat oven 180°C fan forced.

To make pastry: In a medium size mixing bowl combine flour and sugar. Melt margarine and add to milk, using a fork beat egg white into milk mixture until combined. Pour into flour and fold together. Place pastry on a well-floured surface and roll out to fit shape of round pie dish (23cm) that has been coated with cooking spray. Roll up pastry using a rolling pin, lift into pie plate. Trim around edges and bake 10-15 minutes or until lightly browned. Allow to cool.

To make filling: In a medium size saucepan heat all ingredients except milk. Using a whisk, blend ingredients together until mixture comes to the boil, whisk in milk. Leave to cool.

To make meringue: In a medium size mixing bowl beat egg whites until stiff peaks form. Gradually add in sugar beating well each time until all sugar has been used.

To assemble pie: Spread lemon filling evenly over prepared pastry base. Spoon meringue mixture on top of filling, spreading to the edge of pie, make peaks with flat of spoon. Bake 10-15 minutes or until meringue is browned.

Dietitian's Tip
This pie has much less fat than traditional recipes. This is great but the nutrient level is low and the carbohydrate and sugar intake high so I advise people with diabetes to avoid this pie or have it very occasionally.

Nutritional Information

PER SERVE		
FAT	TOTAL	1.0g
	SATURATED	0.3g
FIBRE		0.5g
PROTEIN		3.3g
CARBS		36.1g
SUGAR		25.0g
SODIUM		116mg
KILOJOULES		689 (cals 164)
GI RATING		Medium

Chocolate Trifle

SERVES: 8

1 sachet (9g) diet dark cherry jelly (Cottees®)
1 x 425g can pitted black cherries
100g plain chocolate sponge
60ml port or sherry

CUSTARD MIX

2 cups skim milk
2 tablespoons custard powder
3 tablespoons sugar
1 tablespoon cocoa
½ teaspoon vanilla essence

DIRECTIONS

Make jelly up as directed on packet, refrigerate. Place all the custard mix ingredients into a medium size saucepan, blend with a whisk stirring constantly until mixture boils, leave to cool slightly. Drain cherries and cut in ½. Cut sponge into small pieces and place around base and edge of a deep bowl. Sprinkle port over sponge then place drained cherries on top. Pour custard over cherries. Place in fridge until both custard and jelly have set then mash jelly with a fork until it is mushy, spread evenly over top of custard. Refrigerate until required.

Dietitian's Tip
Something a bit different but offers very little nutritional value.

VARIATION: REPLACE CHERRIES WITH 1 PUNNET FRESH STRAWBERRIES.

Apple Pie

SERVES: 12

2½ cups self-raising flour
¼ cup sugar
¼ cup Flora Light® margarine
½ cup skim milk
1 egg white
flour to roll pastry
cooking spray
1 x 800g can pie apple (no added sugar)
a little skim milk
1 teaspoon sugar

Dietitian's Tip
Annette has made a low fat pastry and used the unsweetened apple as the filling providing lots of vitamins, minerals and fibre making it a nutritious occasional dessert for a person with diabetes.

DIRECTIONS

Preheat oven 180°C fan forced.

In a large mixing bowl combine flour and ¼ cup sugar together. Melt margarine, stir into milk, then using a fork beat egg white into milk mixture until combined. Pour milk mixture into flour and gently fold together. Divide in 2, placing one ½ on a well-floured bench, roll out pastry to fit a round pie dish (23cm). Place rolled pastry over base of pie dish that has been coated with cooking spray. Spread apples evenly over top of pastry. Roll out remaining pastry to fit over top of apple to reach edge of pie dish. Using a sharp knife trim hanging edges. With a fork press edges together, brush top of pastry with a little milk, sprinkle a teaspoon of sugar over top. Bake 40-45 minutes or until golden brown.

Serve with low-fat ice-cream, low-fat custard or low-fat cream.
VARIATIONS: REPLACE APPLE WITH ANY CANNED PIE FRUIT OF YOUR CHOICE
OR TO MAKE A HIGH APPLE PIE USE 2 x 800g CANNED PIE APPLE.

Nutritional Information

PER SERVE		CHERRY	STRAWBERRY
FAT	TOTAL	1.1g	1.1g
	SATURATED	0.3g	0.3g
FIBRE		0.8g	0.8g
PROTEIN		4.3g	4.4g
CARBS		24.7g	19.5g
SUGAR		19.9g	15.1g
SODIUM		72mg	72mg
KILOJOULES		531 (cals 126)	450 (cals 107)
GI RATING		Low	Low

Nutritional Information

PER SERVE		
FAT	TOTAL	2.9g
	SATURATED	0.6g
FIBRE		1.8g
PROTEIN		4.0g
CARBS		33.1g
SUGAR		10.1g
SODIUM		257mg
KILOJOULES		730 (cals 174)
GI RATING		Medium

Baking

Dietitian's Tip: The recipes featured in this section are good alternatives to traditional high-fat baking, however it is important to look at your overall daily intake and try and keep 'extras' and excess kilojoules to a minimum if you wish to obtain good health. This section is high in kilojoules and should be chosen as a treat, not a daily occurrence. The best snack you can have is fruit but when a special occasion arises these recipes are ideal.

Tangy Blueberry Cake

SERVES: 12

CAKE

3 egg whites

⅓ cup sugar

½ teaspoon bicarb soda

½ cup apple sauce (in jar)

2 tablespoons lemon juice

1 tablespoon lemon rind grated

1 teaspoon vanilla essence

½ cup buttermilk

2 cups self-raising flour

1 x 430g can blueberries drained

cooking spray

LEMON ICING (optional)

¾ cup icing sugar

1 teaspoon (5g) Flora Light® margarine

1-2 tablespoons lemon juice

Dietitian's Tip
Have the plain cake without icing if you have diabetes. This not only decreases the sugar content but also the kilojoules and will help with controlling your body weight.

DIRECTIONS

Preheat oven 180ºC fan forced.

In a large mixing bowl beat egg whites and sugar for one minute using an electric beater. Stir bicarb soda into apple sauce (it will froth), add to bowl. Pour lemon juice, rind, essence and buttermilk into mixture and stir together. Gently fold flour into mixture in one go, treat as a sponge, DO NOT BEAT as this will make the cake tough (mixture can look a little lumpy). Gently fold in well-drained blueberries. Pour into a ringed cake tin (19cm) that has been coated with cooking spray. Bake 35-40 minutes or until firm to touch in centre. Allow cake to sit in tin 5 minutes before turning onto a wire rack to cool.

Place icing sugar and margarine into a small mixing bowl, slowly add enough juice to make a spreadable consistency. Sprinkle grated lemon rind over icing for decoration (optional).

Nutritional Information

PER SERVE		PLAIN	ICED
FAT	TOTAL	0.6g	0.8g
	SATURATED	0.2g	0.2g
FIBRE		1.8g	1.8g
PROTEIN		3.9g	3.9g
CARBS		28.2g	36.8g
SUGAR		11.5g	20.0g
SODIUM		208mg	210mg
KILOJOULES		561 (cals 134)	707 (cals 168)
GI RATING		Medium	Medium

Peanut Cookies

MAKES: 15

6 tablespoons (90g) Flora Light® margarine

1 teaspoon vanilla essence

⅓ cup sugar

1 egg white

¼ cup crushed peanuts

1 cup self-raising flour

1 tablespoon skim milk

2 cups corn flakes

cooking spray

DIRECTIONS

Preheat oven 180°C fan forced.

In a large mixing bowl cream margarine, essence and sugar together until sugar has dissolved. Add in egg white and beat until combined. Add peanuts, flour and milk in one go, combine together. Fold corn flakes into mixture, try not to crush. Drop a dessertspoon of mixture onto a baking tray that has been coated with cooking spray. Flatten each cookie a little. Bake 20-25 minutes or until golden brown. Cool on wire rack.

VARIATION: REPLACE CORN FLAKES WITH RICE BUBBLES.

Dietitian's Tip
One cookie contains the same amount of carbohydrate and slightly more kilojoules than a serve of fruit. If you have diabetes you may like to have one but pass on the second.

Nutritional Information

PER COOKIE

FAT	TOTAL	4.1g
	SATURATED	0.7g
FIBRE		0.7g
PROTEIN		2.0g
CARBS		13.7g
SUGAR		4.1g
SODIUM		139mg
KILOJOULES		413 (cals 98)
GI RATING		High

Pumpkin Scones

MAKES: 12

2 egg whites

¼ cup sugar

¼ teaspoon nutmeg

1 tablespoon (15g) Flora Light® margarine

1 cup cooked mashed pumpkin (250g raw)

3 cups self-raising flour

cooking spray

DIRECTIONS

Preheat oven 220°C fan forced.

In a large size mixing bowl beat egg whites and sugar for 1 minute using an electric beater, then add nutmeg. Melt margarine and add to egg mixture, add mashed pumpkin to bowl, stir ingredients together. Gently fold flour into mixture in one go, treat as a sponge, DO NOT BEAT as this will make the scones tough (the less the flour is moved the lighter the scone). This is a fairly moist dough so tip dough onto generously floured surface, generously top with flour and gently knead into dough, pat out and cut 12 scones using a 6cm scone cutter (try not to twist the cutter as this makes the edges tough). Place scones close together onto a baking tray that has been coated with cooking spray. Brush a little skim milk over tops. Bake on top rack 12-15 minutes or until golden brown.

Dietitian's Tip
Scones are a good snack for people with diabetes. However they are usually quite high in carbohydrate and if you decide to add margarine the fat and kilojoule content will increase. Scones are best eaten without a spread.

Nutritional Information

PER SCONE

FAT	TOTAL	1.1g
	SATURATED	0.3g
FIBRE		1.6g
PROTEIN		4.5g
CARBS		29.7g
SUGAR		4.6g
SODIUM		257mg
KILOJOULES		619 (cals 147)
GI RATING		High

Date Slice

MAKES: 20 SLICES

FILLING
2½ cups (300g) seeded dates roughly chopped
2 tablespoons sugar
1 tablespoon lemon juice
1¼ cups water
1 teaspoon bicarb soda
BASE
2½ cups self-raising flour
½ cup rolled oats
¾ cup fresh orange juice
extra flour for rolling
cooking spray

Dietitian's Tip
This product contains quickly absorbed carbohydrate (high glycaemic index) and is best eaten by active people with diabetes when they require a glucose boost.

DIRECTIONS

Preheat oven 180°C fan forced.

To make filling: In a medium size saucepan add dates, sugar, lemon juice and water, bring to boil and simmer 5 minutes, stirring frequently (watch it doesn't burn on base). Add bicarb soda to mixture, beat until fairly smooth. Leave to cool slightly.

To make base: In a large bowl add base ingredients and combine well (the mixture is meant to be quite dry). Divide mixture in 2, use rolling pin and a little flour to roll out one piece until it fits the base of a slab tin, place in tin that has been coated with cooking spray. Spread date filling evenly over top. Roll out remaining piece and place on top of date mixture, brush top with a little milk. Bake 25-30 minutes or until golden brown. Once cooled cut into 20 slices.

VARIATION: REPLACE DATES WITH 2½ CUPS (300g) CHOPPED DRIED APRICOTS AND ADD ¾ CUP MORE OF WATER WHEN COOKING.

Nutritional Information

PER SLICE		DATE	APRICOT
FAT	TOTAL	0.4g	0.4g
	SATURATED	0.1g	0.1g
FIBRE		2.3g	2.2g
PROTEIN		2.3g	2.6g
CARBS		29.8g	26.4g
SUGAR		16.1mg	12.3g
SODIUM		124mg	128g
KILOJOULES		548 (cals 130)	502 (cals 120)
GI RATING		Medium	Medium

Apple Sultana Teacake

SERVES: 8

2 egg whites
¼ cup sugar
½ teaspoon bicarb soda
½ cup apple sauce (in jar)
1 cup peeled apple finely diced
½ cup sultanas
⅓ cup skim milk
2 cups self-raising flour
cooking spray
3 teaspoons sugar
1 teaspoon cinnamon

Dietitian's Tip
Lots of carbohydrate in this cake making it an unsuitable snack or dessert for many people with diabetes.

DIRECTIONS

Preheat oven 180°C fan forced.

In a large mixing bowl beat egg whites and sugar for 1 minute using an electric beater. Stir bicarb soda into apple sauce (it will froth) then add to bowl. Add chopped apple, sultanas, milk and combine. Gently fold flour into mixture in one go, treat as a sponge, DO NOT BEAT as this will make the cake tough. Pour mixture into a round cake tin (19cm) that has been coated with cooking spray. Mix 3 teaspoons sugar and 1 teaspoon cinnamon together then sprinkle over top of cake batter. Bake 30-35 minutes or until firm to touch in centre. Allow cake to sit 5 minutes in tin before turning onto a wire rack to cool.

VARIATIONS: OMIT SULTANAS AND APPLE FOR A PLAIN TEACAKE OR REPLACE SULTANAS WITH CURRANTS OR CHOPPED DRIED APRICOTS OR REPLACE CHOPPED APPLE WITH CHOPPED FRESH PEAR.

Nutritional Information

PER SERVE		
FAT	TOTAL	0.4g
	SATURATED	0.1g
FIBRE		1.7g
PROTEIN		4.1g
CARBS		36.9g
SUGAR		16.7g
SODIUM		242mg
KILOJOULES		701 (cals 167)
GI RATING		Medium

Royal Easter Show 2001
1st prize

Wicked Chocolate Cake

SERVES: 12

CAKE

¾ cup caster sugar

4 tablespoons (60g) Flora Light® margarine

¾ cup boiling water

1¼ cups self-raising flour

½ teaspoon bicarb soda

¼ cup cocoa

2 egg whites

cooking spray

ICING

¾ cup icing sugar

1 tablespoon cocoa

1-1½ tablespoons skim milk

Nutritional Information

PER SERVE		ICED	W/OUT ICING
FAT	TOTAL	3.0g	2.9g
	SATURATED	0.7g	0.7g
FIBRE		0.7g	0.6g
PROTEIN		2.5g	2.4g
CARBS		32.0g	23.2g
SUGAR		21.2g	12.6g
SODIUM		160mg	157mg
KILOJOULES		676 (cals 161)	531 (cals 126)
GI RATING		Medium	Medium

DIRECTIONS

In a medium size mixing bowl completely dissolve sugar and margarine in boiling water. Sift flour, bicarb and cocoa into bowl in one go, using an electric beater beat together 1 minute, add egg whites and beat 30 seconds more. Using a microwave round ring dish (6 cup) or a microwave dish that has a separate centre piece, coat with cooking spray, cut out grease proof paper to fit base of dish and line base, spray top of paper with cooking spray, coat centre piece with cooking spray and place in middle. Pour cake mix into dish and place in centre of microwave. For a 650 watt cook 6 minutes on HIGH. For a 1000 watt cook 4 minutes on HIGH. For a 1200 watt cook 3 minutes 40 seconds on HIGH. Leave in microwave 2 minutes then remove, turn out on cake rack, peel off paper and cool.

Once cake has cooled, place all icing ingredients into a small mixing bowl and combine well. Spread icing evenly over top.

VARIATION:
TO MAKE IN CONVENTIONAL OVEN FOLLOW RECIPE BUT INSTEAD OF USING A MICROWAVE DISH USE A RINGED METAL CAKE TIN COATED WITH COOKING SPRAY. BAKE IN FAN-FORCED OVEN 180°C FOR APPROXIMATELY 30 MINUTES.

Dietitian's Tip
Everyones favourite but this cake offers little nutritional value to your diet.

Peppermint Bubble Bar

MAKES: 16 SLICES

BASE

2 x 40g peppermint bars (Darrell Lea®)

4 tablespoons (60g) Flora Light® margarine

1 tablespoon golden syrup

3 cups rice bubbles

cooking spray

ICING

1¼ cups icing sugar

2 tablespoons cocoa

2 tablespoons skim milk

¼ teaspoon peppermint essence

DIRECTIONS

Roughly chop peppermint bars then place bars, margarine and golden syrup in microwave-safe bowl and melt on high for 2 minutes, stir well and microwave a further 1 minute, beat mixture until smooth. In a large mixing bowl add in rice bubbles, pour in melted chocolate mix and stir together well until rice bubbles are all covered with chocolate mix. Coat a slab tin with cooking spray and press mixture into tin evenly. Refrigerate. Once cold make icing. In a small mixing bowl add all icing ingredients and mix together well, (if too thick add a little more milk). Spread icing over base and refrigerate. Once set cut into 16 slices.

Dietitian's Tip

A real treat but has very little nutritional value.

Nutritional Information

PER SLICE		
FAT	TOTAL	2.6g
	SATURATED	0.8g
FIBRE		0.1g
PROTEIN		0.6g
CARBS		20.4g
SUGAR		16.1g
SODIUM		80mg
KILOJOULES		441 (cals 105)
GI RATING		High

Citrus Poppyseed Cake

SERVES: 12

CAKE

2 egg whites

⅓ cup sugar

½ teaspoon bicarb soda

½ cup apple sauce (in jar)

1 cup cooked mashed pumpkin (250g raw)

½ cup fresh orange or lemon juice

1 tablespoon orange or lemon rind

½ teaspoon vanilla essence

3 tablespoons poppy seeds

2 cups self-raising flour

cooking spray

ICING

¾ cup icing sugar

1 tablespoon orange or lemon juice

grated orange or lemon rind for decoration

1 teaspoon (5g) Flora Light® margarine

DIRECTIONS

Preheat oven 180°C fan forced.

In a medium size mixing bowl beat egg whites and sugar for 1 minute using an electric beater. Stir bicarb soda into apple sauce (it will froth) then add to bowl. Mix in cooked pumpkin, juice, rind, essence and poppy seeds. Gently fold flour into mixture in one go, treat as a sponge, DO NOT BEAT as this will make the cake tough. Pour mixture into a round cake tin (19cm) that has been coated with cooking spray. Bake 35-40 minutes or until firm to touch in centre. Allow cake to sit 5 minutes in tin before turning onto a wire rack to cool.

ICING: Once cake has cooled place all icing ingredients into a small mixing bowl, blend together until smooth (if too stiff add a few drops more of juice). Spread over top of cake. Sprinkle rind or a few poppy seeds over icing for decoration.

NOTE:
In hot, humid weather it is best to keep this cake refrigerated.

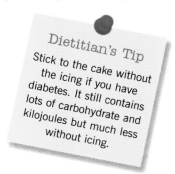

Dietitian's Tip
Stick to the cake without the icing if you have diabetes. It still contains lots of carbohydrate and kilojoules but much less without icing.

Nutritional Information

PER SERVE		WITH ICING	W/OUT ICING
FAT	TOTAL	1.5g	1.3g
	SATURATED	0.3g	0.2g
FIBRE		1.6g	1.6g
PROTEIN		3.8g	3.8g
CARBS		34.8g	26.0g
SUGAR		17.5g	8.8g
SODIUM		200mg	197mg
KILOJOULES		699 (cals 166)	551 (cals 131)
GI RATING		Medium	Medium

Apricot and Almond Muffins

MAKES: 10

cooking spray
¾ cup dried apricots chopped
½ teaspoon bicarb soda
1 cup (250ml) boiling water
2 egg whites
⅓ cup sugar
¾ teaspoon almond essence
2 cups self-raising flour
20g blanched almond flakes

Dietitian's Tip
This snack contains about the same carbohydrate and kilojoules as a bread roll or two slices of bread. People with diabetes may like to have this as their breakfast with low fat milk or a fruit juice.

DIRECTIONS

Preheat oven 180°C fan forced.

Coat a 12 cup muffin tin with cooking spray. Mix together apricots, bicarb soda and water in a small mixing bowl, let stand for 15 minutes. Beat egg whites and sugar together in a medium size mixing bowl for 1 minute. Add almond essence and apricots to egg mixture. Gently fold flour into mixture in one go, treat as a sponge, DO NOT BEAT as this will make the muffins tough. Once ingredients are just combined spoon mixture into prepared muffin pans, dividing equally into 10 cups. Sprinkle almond flakes over tops of muffins then bake in oven for 15-20 minutes or until cooked.

Nutritional Information

PER MUFFIN		
FAT	TOTAL	1.5g
	SATURATED	0.1g
FIBRE		2.2g
PROTEIN		4.3g
CARBS		30.2g
SUGAR		10.1g
SODIUM		237mg
KILOJOULES		634 (cals 151)
GI RATING		Medium

Savoury Muffins

MAKES: 10

cooking spray
2 egg whites
½ teaspoon bicarb soda
⅓ cup apple sauce (in jar)
½ cup raw pumpkin grated
⅓ cup carrot grated
⅓ cup onion finely diced
⅓ cup frozen peas
⅓ cup frozen corn kernels
⅓ cup red capsicum diced
1 x 200g tub low-fat natural yoghurt
2 tablespoons grated parmesan cheese
1 cup unprocessed bran
pepper to taste
2 cups self-raising flour

Dietitian's Tip
Many savory muffins are very high in fat and kilojoules. This recipe recommends the use of low fat products resulting in it having less kilojoules than traditional muffins making it a suitable occasional food for people with diabetes.

DIRECTIONS

Preheat oven 200°C fan forced.

Coat a 12 cup muffin tin with cooking spray. In a large mixing bowl beat egg whites for one minute using an electric beater. Add bicarb soda to apple sauce (it will froth) then add to bowl. Stir in all vegetables, yoghurt, parmesan cheese, bran, pepper and combine. Gently fold flour into mixture in one go, treat as a sponge, DO NOT BEAT as this will make the muffins tough (mixture can look a little lumpy). Spoon mixture into prepared muffin tin, dividing equally into 10 cups. Bake 20 minutes or until firm to touch in centre. Allow muffins to sit in pan 5 minutes before turning onto a wire rack to cool.

Nutritional Information

PER MUFFIN		
FAT	TOTAL	1.3g
	SATURATED	0.5g
FIBRE		4.6g
PROTEIN		7.0g
CARBS		26.1g
SUGAR		4.1g
SODIUM		274mg
KILOJOULES		614 (cals 146)
GI RATING		Medium

Blueberry and Banana Muffins

MAKES: 10

cooking spray

2 egg whites

¼ cup sugar

½ teaspoon bicarb soda

½ cup apple sauce (in jar)

½ cup mashed ripe banana

2½ cups self-raising flour

1 cup canned blueberries (well drained)

DIRECTIONS

Preheat oven 200ºC fan forced.

Coat a 12 cup muffin tin with cooking spray. In a medium size mixing bowl beat egg whites and sugar for 1 minute using an electric beater. Stir bicarb soda into apple sauce (it will froth) then add to bowl. Place mashed banana into bowl and mix together. Gently fold flour into mixture in one go, treat as a sponge, DO NOT BEAT, as this will make the muffins tough (mixture can look a little lumpy). Gently fold blueberries into mixture. Spoon into prepared muffin tin dividing equally into 10 cups. Bake 15-20 minutes or until firm to touch in centre. Allow muffins to sit 5 minutes in tin before turning onto a wire rack to cool.

VARIATIONS: REPLACE BANANA WITH CHOPPED FRESH APPLE OR CHOPPED FRESH PEAR.

Dietitian's Tip
This snack contains about the same carbohydrate and kilojoules as a bread roll or two slices of bread. People with diabetes may like to have this as their breakfast with low fat milk or a fruit juice.

Easy Fruit Muffins

MAKES: 12

1 cup mixed fruit

1 cup fruit medley

½ teaspoon bicarb soda

1 teaspoon mixed spice

2 cups boiling tea (strong)

2 cups self-raising flour

cooking spray

Dietitian's Tip
Lots of carbohydrate, vitamins, minerals and fibre in these muffins making them ideal for athletic, active people with diabetes.

DIRECTIONS

Preheat oven 180°C fan forced.

Combine fruits, bicarb, mixed spice and tea, leave to soak for 15 minutes. Gently fold flour into mixture in one go, treat as a sponge, DO NOT BEAT as this will make the muffins tough. Coat a 12 cup muffin tin with cooking spray and spoon mixture into muffin tin, dividing equally into 12 cups. Bake 20 minutes or until firm to touch in centre. Allow muffins to sit 5 minutes in tin before turning out onto a wire rack to cool.

Nutritional Information

PER MUFFIN

FAT	TOTAL	0.4g
	SATURATED	0.1g
FIBRE		2.1g
PROTEIN		3.8g
CARBS		32.0g
SUGAR		10.8g
SODIUM		237mg
KILOJOULES		617 (cals 147)
GI RATING		Medium

Nutritional Information

PER MUFFIN

FAT	TOTAL	0.5g
	SATURATED	0.1g
FIBRE		2.5g
PROTEIN		2.8g
CARBS		32.3g
SUGAR		13.4g
SODIUM		197mg
KILOJOULES		594 (cals 141)
GI RATING		Low

Best Ever Muffins

MAKES: 12

cooking spray
2 egg whites
¼ cup brown sugar (loosely packed)
½ teaspoon bicarb soda
½ cup apple sauce (in jar)
½ cup carrot grated
¼ cup sultanas
¼ cup currants
1 small apple peeled and diced
¼ cup rolled oats
½ cup low-fat natural yoghurt
1 cup self-raising wholemeal flour
1 cup self-raising flour

Dietitian's Tip
Lots of carbohydrate, vitamins, minerals and fibre in these muffins making them ideal for athletic, active people with diabetes.

DIRECTIONS

Preheat oven 200°C fan forced.

Coat a 12 cup muffin tin with cooking spray. In a large size mixing bowl beat egg whites and sugar for 1 minute using an electric beater. Stir bicarb soda into apple sauce (it will froth) then add to bowl. Add carrot, sultanas, currants, apple, oats and yoghurt mixing ingredients together well. Gently fold flours into mixture in one go, treat as a sponge, DO NOT BEAT as this will make the muffins tough (mixture can look a little lumpy). Spoon mixture into prepared muffin pan, dividing equally into 12 cups. Bake 15-20 minutes or until firm to touch in centre. Allow muffins to sit 5 minutes in tin before turning onto a wire rack to cool.

Nutritional Information

PER MUFFIN		
FAT	TOTAL	0.7g
	SATURATED	0.1g
FIBRE		3.1g
PROTEIN		4.6g
CARBS		33.8g
SUGAR		17.4g
SODIUM		214mg
KILOJOULES		668 (cals 159)
GI RATING		Medium

Boysenberry and Apple Muffins

MAKES: 12

cooking spray
2 egg whites
¼ cup sugar
½ teaspoon bicarb soda
½ cup apple sauce (in jar)
½ cup peeled apple diced
2½ cups self-raising flour
1 x 425g can boysenberries (well drained)

DIRECTIONS

Preheat oven 200°C fan forced.

Coat a 12 cup muffin tin with cooking spray. In a medium size mixing bowl beat egg whites and sugar for 1 minute using an electric beater. Stir bicarb soda into apple sauce (it will froth) then add to bowl. Place chopped apple into bowl and mix ingredients together. Gently fold flour into mixture in one go, treat as a sponge, DO NOT BEAT as this will make the muffins tough (mixture can look a little lumpy). Gently fold boysenberries into mixture, spoon into prepared muffin tin, dividing equally into 12 cups. Bake 15-20 minutes or until firm to touch in centre. Allow muffins to sit for 5 minutes in tin before turning onto a wire rack to cool.

VARIATIONS: REPLACE CHOPPED APPLE WITH FRESH PEAR OR MASHED BANANA.

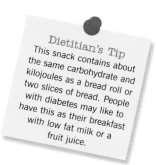

Dietitian's Tip
This snack contains about the same carbohydrate and kilojoules as a bread roll or two slices of bread. People with diabetes may like to have this as their breakfast with low fat milk or a fruit juice.

Nutritional Information

PER MUFFIN		
FAT	TOTAL	0.4g
	SATURATED	0.1g
FIBRE		2.0g
PROTEIN		3.7g
CARBS		30.6g
SUGAR		9.7g
SODIUM		237mg
KILOJOULES		591 (cals 141)
GI RATING		Medium

Golden Wheat Slice

MAKES: 15 SLICES

SLICE

cooking spray

1 cup self-raising flour

4 crushed Weet-Bix®

½ cup sultanas (optional)

⅓ cup brown sugar (firmly packed)

6 tablespoons (90g) Flora Light® margarine

1 tablespoon golden syrup

2 tablespoons skim milk

ICING

1 cup icing sugar

1 tablespoon lemon juice

1 tablespoon skim milk

1 teaspoon (5g) Flora Light® margarine

DIRECTIONS

Preheat oven 180°C fan forced.

Coat a slab tin with cooking spray. In a medium size mixing bowl combine flour, crushed Weet-Bix®, sultanas and brown sugar. Melt margarine in microwave for 30 seconds, add the golden syrup and milk mixing together. Pour margarine mixture into dry ingredients and combine well. Press mixture evenly over base of slab tin that has been coated with cooking spray (using your hand). Bake 20-25 minutes or until browned.

ICING: In a small mixing bowl mix icing ingredients together until smooth, pour icing over hot slice, leave to cool. Cut when cold.

Dietitian's Tip
Forget the icing if you have diabetes.

Fruit and Oat Bread

SERVES: 12

¼ cup rolled oats

1¼ cups water

2 egg whites

⅓ cup sugar

¾ cup mixed fruit

½ teaspoon nutmeg

½ teaspoon cinnamon

2½ cups self-raising flour

cooking spray

DIRECTIONS

Preheat oven 180°C fan forced.

In a small saucepan cook oats and water until porridge is made (should equal 1 cup cooked). In a large mixing bowl beat egg whites and sugar with electric beater for one minute. Add mixed fruit, spices and prepared porridge combining together well. Gently fold flour into mixture in one go, treat as a sponge, DO NOT BEAT as this will make the bread tough. Pour into a loaf tin that has been coated with cooking spray. Bake 35-40 minutes or until firm to touch in centre. Allow loaf to sit 5 minutes in tin before turning onto a wire rack to cool.

Dietitian's Tip
Contains lots of slowly absorbed carbohydrate and plenty of vitamins, minerals and fibre making it an ideal breakfast bread for people with diabetes

Nutritional Information

PER SLICE		
FAT	TOTAL	3.1g
	SATURATED	0.6g
FIBRE		0.7g
PROTEIN		1.4g
CARBS		21.5g
SUGAR		13.2g
SODIUM		103mg
KILOJOULES		493 (cals 117)
GI RATING		Medium

Nutritional Information

PER SERVE		
FAT	TOTAL	0.7g
	SATURATED	0.1g
FIBRE		1.9g
PROTEIN		4.0g
CARBS		34.6g
SUGAR		11.8g
SODIUM		220mg
KILOJOULES		674 (cals 160)
GI RATING		Medium

Pineapple Fruit Cake

SERVES: 16

3 cups (500g) mixed dried fruit

1 teaspoon mixed spice

⅓ cup water

1 x 440g crushed pineapple (in natural juice)

¾ teaspoon bicarb soda

3 egg whites

2 cups self-raising flour

cooking spray

DIRECTIONS

In a medium size saucepan place mixed fruit, spice, water and the whole can of pineapple, bring to boil, simmer for 3 minutes. Stir in bicarb soda, leave to cool.

Preheat oven 180°C fan forced.

Once fruit mixture has cooled beat egg whites into fruit mixture well. Gently fold flour into mixture in one go. Pour mixture into a round cake tin (19cm) or large loaf tin that has been coated with cooking spray and bake approximately 1 hour. Allow cake to sit 5 minutes in tin before turning onto a wire rack to cool.

Dietitian's Tip
This recipe contains lots of carbohydrate and kilojoules but also has a high nutritional value. Many people with diabetes may find that this is not suitable for them.

Nutritional Information

PER SERVE		
FAT	TOTAL	0.5g
	SATURATED	0.1g
FIBRE		2.8g
PROTEIN		3.1g
CARBS		35.6g
SUGAR		22.7g
SODIUM		191mg
KILOJOULES		660 (cals 157)
GI RATING		Low

Zucci Walnut Cake

SERVES: 12

Dietitian's Tip
This cake contains vegetables, fruit and nuts and therefore lots of carbohydrate, some protein and "healthy" fats. If you have diabetes avoid the extra sugar and try it without the icing.

CAKE

2 egg whites

¼ cup sugar

½ teaspoon bicarb soda

½ cup apple sauce (in jar)

¼ cup walnuts chopped

½ cup currants

½ cup zucchini grated (packed firm)

½ cup crushed pineapple (in natural juice) drained

¾ teaspoon mixed spice

2 cups self-raising flour

cooking spray

ICING (optional)

¾ cup icing sugar

1-1½ tablespoons pineapple juice

1 teaspoon (5g) Flora Light® margarine

DIRECTIONS

Preheat oven 180°C fan forced.

In a medium size mixing bowl beat egg whites and sugar for 1 minute using an electric beater. Stir bicarb into apple sauce (it will froth) then add to bowl. Add walnuts, currants, zucchini, pineapple and mixed spice to bowl, combine all ingredients together. Gently fold flour into mixture in one go, treat as a sponge, DO NOT BEAT as this will make the cake tough. Pour mixture into a round cake tin (19cm) that has been coated with cooking spray. Bake 35-40 minutes or until firm to touch in centre. Allow cake to sit 5 minutes in tin before turning onto a wire rack to cool. Once cake has cooled place all icing ingredients into a small mixing bowl, combine well. Spread over top of cake.

Nutritional Information

PER SERVE		ICED	W/OUT ICING
FAT	TOTAL	2.0g	1.8g
	SATURATED	0.2g	0.1g
FIBRE		1.6g	1.6g
PROTEIN		3.5g	3.5g
CARBS		36.1g	27.4g
SUGAR		19.3g	10.6g
SODIUM		201mg	199mg
KILOJOULES		733 (cals 174)	585 (cals 139)
GI RATING		Medium	Medium

Index

If you would like Annette to come and speak at your group, conference or seminar please phone:

The Symply Too Good To Be True Hotline (07) 5445 1250 (Int: +61 7 5445 1250)
Annette's Web Site - www.symplytoogood.com.au

Annette's cookbooks are sold in all good newsagents throughout Australia.

For information on stockists phone/fax the hotline or email: asym@bigpond.net.au